December 25, 1986

Dear Elizabeth,

This book is to share with your family this year. I think you will enjoy the short stories and their messages of inspiration.

We will miss being here at Christmas time but, our thoughts will be with you. And we will be doing what we believe the Lord wants us to do.

We love you and pray that everything will go well while we are away.

Love from both of us.

Dad

The Outstretched Arms

More Stories of Courage,
Conviction, and Love

Kris Mackay

Bookcraft · Salt Lake City, Utah

To
my Father and Mother
Barney and Katie Kristofferson
whose whole lives have been
examples
of courage, conviction,
and love

Library of Congress Catalog Card Number: 83-62417
ISBN O-88494-501-4

First Printing, 1983

Lithographed in the United States of America
PUBLISHERS PRESS
Salt Lake City, Utah

Contents

1
The Outstretched Arms

Very few places on earth are colder than Norway in the winter. My father — Bjarne then, Barney now — was born there. He was six years old when his family moved to Ogden, Utah. My brother, Don, was the first Kristofferson to return.

Elders Donald Kristofferson and Calvin Broadhead readjusted the collars of their heavy overcoats and hunched their shoulders into the icy Arctic wind. They were tracting in the city of Bergen on the western shores of Norway, systematically tracting in one particular area, using maps to be certain no house was overlooked.

They started up a long, steep flight of outdoor stairs toward a house balanced at the top of the hill, their boots crunching on the hard-packed snow. They reached the house and found it was not part of the street they were methodically covering. Actually, it faced a different direction and belonged to the street above. Strictly speaking, they needn't have made the effort.

But they had climbed the steps and were standing, shivering, just outside the front door. It would be a long time before they tracted this way again. (As it turned out, they never did.) They might as well knock.

Fru Anna Berg opened the door, a large, big-boned, pleasant Norwegian woman. She kindly invited them in to warm themselves at her fire, but she laughed, "I want you to know I don't believe in your church."

They enjoyed the visit thoroughly. She was friendly and intelligent and an avid Bible scholar. Every room in her home held its own Bible and not one of them gathered dust. She was a humble woman—not timid, certainly, even outspoken, but humble in her determined search for truth.

Once in a while missionaries are fortunate to locate a contact so golden that teaching is hardly necessary. So it was with this good woman. The Anderson discussion plan was in use then and it was heavily laced with scripture, ideal material for someone so unusually familiar with the Bible.

Fru Berg's thoughtful study of scripture over a lifetime had prepared her with an accurate personal picture of the plan of salvation. Each time the missionaries introduced a topic, *she* outlined it to *them*, in ways compatible with doctrine they expected to teach to her.

The one concept she couldn't accept at that point was that Joseph Smith had been visited by God the Father and his Son Jesus Christ. The two young men suggested she take the matter to the Lord in prayer. She did, and she was excited by the confirmation she received. Before they saw her again, she was enthusiastically explaining the visitation to her friends.

Her progress stumbled, briefly, for a second time when the Elders quoted from 1 Corinthians 15:29: "Else what shall they do which are baptized for the dead, if the dead rise not at all?"

Despite her comprehensive knowledge of scripture, this passage had escaped her attention. She had difficulty in grasping the reasoning behind baptism for the dead. Again she was counseled to pray for understanding, and again the principle was made clear to her as a comforting, basic truth.

Both missionaries sensed she was near whole-hearted belief. But suddenly they were transferred from the city. Elder Kristofferson's last few months passed quickly, and his mission came to an end. He would leave for home from the capital city of Oslo, so he started a day or two early, stopped on the way in Bergen, "borrowed" a local companion, and went with him to the home of Fru Berg.

It was a joyful reunion. A very, very special love exists between the investigator who at long last discovers the previously hidden path of truth and the missionary who stood as a beacon at the crossroads, pointing out the way. She teetered, she knew, on the verge of a momentous decision, and she entreated the Elder to stay in Bergen just a little while longer.

His answer was, "Fru Berg, I'm due in Oslo tomorrow. Only one thing could make it possible for me to stay beyond today."

He referred to her baptism, but he didn't really understand what he was asking. Intellectually she was ready. She wanted it. But she was also desperately afraid.

A severe heart condition she'd never mentioned to the Elders made her susceptible to sudden shocks or chills. They could, and probably would, be fatal. Consequently she was in mortal fear of the baptismal process of immersion.

The chapel in Bergen occupied the second floor of a three-story building. The ground floor housed retail shops and the third story was set up as living quarters during missionary language training courses. A small kitchen adjoined the living quarters.

The baptismal font was uniquely situated beneath floorboards of the chapel, out of sight when not in use. Removal of a small section of flooring behind the podium revealed stairs which led directly down into the font.

A nearby heater warmed the building's water supply, so Elder Kristofferson foresaw no difficulty when he promised

Fru Berg the water would be comfortably warm. He would see
to it personally.

He hurried to the chapel several hours early the next
morning. Every detail had to be perfect. Interviews with the
branch president had been completed the previous evening.
The ceremony was scheduled for 1:00 P.M.

He checked for hot water. There wasn't any. The water
heater was broken! It was completely nonfunctional, and the
weather outside was still extremely cold.

No one had ever told him that working for the Lord would
be easy. He rounded up other Elders and they frantically
raced the clock to boil water on the small third-floor-kitchen
stove in pots and pans normally used for cooking.

Then they careened down the narrow staircase at top speed
and across the chapel, trying their best to hold the pans steady
and minimize sloshing until the heated water could be thrown
into the font. It went in with approximately the impact of
drops of rain joining the mighty Atlantic Ocean.

They made more trips than they cared to count. Each
panful they added to the cold water flowing in through the
pipes caused the surface level to inch upwards and—*please,
God!*—would remove the chill.

Elder Kristofferson understood his friend's deep-seated
fear, but he also understood and felt the strength of her long-
ing to comply with what her Heavenly Father required of her.
Because of trust in him as the Lord's commissioned representative, she had succeeded in gaining the upper hand over
paralyzing foreboding. If he left Bergen with her goal un-
realized, could she find the necessary courage to make a
second attempt?

The water at last reached a satisfactory level and he busied
himself with other arrangements.

A few minutes before one, he went back to the font. He
plunged his right arm deep down into the water—and found it
was bitterly cold! The missionaries' exhausting efforts hadn't
been enough. The water they'd boiled in the kitchen and

carried down with such high hopes had reverted to its original icy temperature.

He prayed then as hard as he has ever prayed in his life, before or since. Stewardship for his friend's physical and spiritual lives rested in his hands. He felt like a juggler who is unexpectedly called upon to juggle two priceless, irreplaceable jewels, and by catching hold of one of them risks dropping the other through his fingers to its destruction. Help from a higher power was needed in this awesome responsibility.

He didn't hear a voice or see a vision, but he was strongly, unmistakably impressed to proceed. He couldn't believe that a woman who desired membership in the kingdom as sincerely as she did could be harmed in the waters of baptism. He and others had exerted every effort to make her comfortable and safe. Surely the Lord would protect and be with her.

He waited for Fru Berg to join him in the chapel. When she arrived, he preceded her down the stairs and into the font. He was delighted to find the water now pleasantly warm to his body, not frigid as when it had touched his arm a few minutes before, and he accepted the warmth gratefully as a literal answer to his prayers.

He smiled to offer reassurance to the frightened woman, but she was staring past him. His hand reached up to help her descend, but she didn't stir.

He spoke to her, asking for her full name, but there was no response.

He spoke to her a second time. There was not the slightest sign that she heard his voice. She appeared to be as detached as if turned to stone.

Apparently fear was victorious.

When Anna Berg closed the door behind Elder Kristofferson the night before, her attitude wasn't nearly as positive as she'd led him to believe it was. She'd confided her fear of physical trauma or death at the moment of immersion, but she hadn't confessed the real, more complex anxiety.

Baptism was not new to her. As an infant she was accepted into the state church in that manner. Later on she became convinced that infant baptism is not a proper procedure in the sight of the Lord; she believed one should reach an age of accountability prior to that important commitment. Thereafter she searched diligently for a church which espoused the doctrine of delayed baptism.

She found such a creed and eagerly submitted to a second ceremony—before delving as deeply as perhaps she should have into their other beliefs. Most of them didn't match hers.

Eagerness turned to frustration, despair, and a sense of personal guilt. In her rush to do what was right, she had relied solely on her own powers of deduction. She hadn't waited for direction from the Spirit. She passionately vowed she would never, *never* make that mistake again!

Stirred as she was by the message of the restored gospel, now her feelings went beyond hope. She had felt inner whisperings of the Spirit and deeply believed she was doing what the Lord wanted of her, and yet she knew she couldn't afford the luxury of another mistake.

She truly believed that another disappointment *would* be fatal to her weakened heart, more surely than the shock of ice-cold water to her body.

This time she didn't ask just for a whispering. She prayed for knowledge. She had to know. She was willing to offer up her mortal life if that's what it took, but she had to know that this baptism was the Savior's will.

The night before the baptism she prayed without ceasing all night long. The first rays of morning light broke through her window and still the heavens were mute.

She left home and wandered aimlessly, pleading with all the strength of her soul.

At 12:45 P.M. she found herself standing in front of the church. Confused, she went inside, dressed in white, then met Elder Kristofferson in the chapel.

She loved him and trusted his word, but without an answer from the Lord she couldn't relinquish her terror. By taking his hand and going with him into the water, she would literally be walking to her death.

Elder Kristofferson repeated his request for her name a third time. This time she answered.

She stirred and the dazed look left her face. The look was replaced by a glowing radiance he'd never seen there before.

She reached out for his hand and stepped confidently down the stairs. The firmness of her grasp and quickness of her step let him know she was no longer afraid. Immobilizing terror had evaporated like morning mist when greeted by the light of the sun.

Her baptism went smoothly and there were no ill effects. She was confirmed right there at the edge of the water, and only then did Elder Kristofferson hear the explanation for her miraculous change in behavior.

She had no idea how long she had stood on the stairs, transfixed, but in those few moments, sacred beyond her wildest imaginings, she received her answer and knew what she should do.

At the far edge of the font, a step behind and to the left of the waiting Elder, she saw a figure robed in white, and his outstretched arms took away hesitation and fear.

They spoke to her as plainly as if his mouth had uttered the words. And their message was: "Come unto me."

2
The Lord's Lease

Mark and Ada Hardman were reared in diametrically opposite styles in the homes of their parents.

Mark's family was inflexible in demanding full attendance at all church functions. There was no acceptable excuse for staying at home.

Ada's parents were much more lenient. Her brothers and sisters were blessed and baptized, but attendance from then on was left up to each child's individual preference.

Two extreme philosophies, yet they fostered the same negative result. Mark's inclination was to convince himself and his parents that he did have a right to independence, and Ada didn't consider regularity of worship to be important. They had only sporadic contact with organized religion in their early married years, and the study of religious principles held low priority in their busy schedules.

But the picturesque endearment "salt of the earth" might have been coined expressly for them. It fit them both to a *T*.

Good, solid, hard-working, dependable people who raised three children to honorable adulthood and whose children, in turn, presented them with ten beautiful grandchildren.

By then they figured the pattern of their lives was set and they looked forward to no major modifications. The last thing they expected was to be called on a stake mission.

They were ranchers, not students of scripture. They had finally thrown off the yokes of their parents' referred animosities and for the past five years had been as active in the Church as anyone could wish. They tried to do whatever their leaders asked of them, to compensate for all the lost years.

But a call to fill a mission was ridiculous and out of the question! How could they teach the intricate beauties of God's truths with enough assurance and skill to touch the heart of an investigator? There were still too many fine points to look up and clarify for themselves.

Nevertheless they accepted the call, and that's how they came to be standing outside their first missionary door. They were tracting. And they were sick with nervous apprehension.

Mark raised his hand to knock, then drew it back. They still had time to back away. Like good missionaries everywhere, they carried a prayer in their hearts, but this was the essence of their particular prayer: "Dear, kind Father, *please* don't let anyone be home!"

Mark rapped timidly. The door swung open immediately to reveal a jovial gentleman a few years older than he, and in his hand the man carried an open Bible.

"Come in! Come in! You're just in time!" he invited, as if they were expected and had knocked exactly on schedule.

Leading the way into a modest living room, he introduced them to his wife and waved his hand over an end table loaded down with open scriptures of various kinds.

"We have something we'd like you folks to clear up for us," their host continued. "We've discussed our confusion with Bible students of every denomination except yours, and nobody has come up with an answer."

So saying, he bent over the waiting books. He moistened his finger and flipped pages back and forth in search of the elusive quotation.

Mark and Ada turned pale. Ada thought she might faint. They had convinced themselves that if the conversations were kept simple, they might manage. What had they stumbled into?

Mark cleared his throat. He said authoritatively, "One moment, please. We never discuss any subject until after prayer."

Then like a condemned prisoner looking longingly toward a reprieve, he began to pray. He stretched the exhortations out for as long as he dared before closing the prayer and opening his eyes.

The gentleman posed his question. The Hardmans had no idea what the answer was, and for a few seconds his words hung, quivering, in the air between them.

Then Mark began to answer. He was as astonished as his wife was at the authority of the explanations leaving his lips. He quoted chapter and verse, looked them up, and the question was answered. His comments satisfied the other couple completely.

That satisfied the Hardmans too, and they relaxed. They were hard-working people. If they studied with all their might and asked for help, that help would be with them when it was needed. With that assurance, their mission took on deeper meaning.

Stake guidelines suggested they devote ten hours a week to the work. But before long things got out of hand. Investigators brought friends who, next time around, brought friends of their own. The down-to-earth honesty of this special couple inspired confidence. They were swamped with investigators.

Trying to keep pace, Mark and Ada scheduled meetings every night of the week and frequently sandwiched in two meetings the same night. They loved those teaching hours.

Getting home to the ranch exhausted at eleven or twelve at night, however, wasn't nearly as enjoyable, since Mark still had chores to do and cattle to bed down at that impossible hour.

One night Mark spoke to his wife about the problem after a particularly tiring day. "Ada," he said regretfully, "this isn't working. We've got to sit down and make a decision."

Running the ranch was a full-time job, and as it was turning out, so was their mission. Contenting themselves with doing anything halfway wasn't their style, and they couldn't start hedging now. Either they must sell the ranch or ask to be released from their mission.

Sitting across from each other over the dining room table, they soberly considered all angles. Their productive working years were nearing an end. All their lives had been a struggle to build financial independence for retirement. Cattle prices were down that year; it was a terrible time to sell. And to risk winding up as burdens to their children wouldn't be fair.

Even so their hearts were drawn back to their mission, and they realized they loved it even more than they'd known. In spite of every practical argument to the contrary, they couldn't face giving it up.

They went to bed that night with heavy hearts, but agreed to sleep on it before making the final decision.

Mark slipped quietly out of bed very early the next morning, dressed, and hurried out to an outlying field. He wasn't ready with his decision.

Their property fronted along the highway and the house sat back a quarter of a mile from the road. Out in the field, he didn't notice the black, expensive car turning into their private lane at mid-morning. Ada did, and she stepped onto the porch to greet the stranger who pulled to a stop in their driveway.

The man presented her with an interesting business proposal. Would she and her husband consider leasing their ranch?

He and his partner had been on the lookout for a showplace to exhibit their special breed of cattle. The Hardman ranch ran adjacent to the highway, making their spread the ideal spot. The company didn't wish to purchase outright because—strangely enough—they needed the ranch for a period of only two years.

The man apologized profusely for the intrusion. He would be back the following day for their answer.

Mark sat up past midnight that night surrounded by financial record books. Using last year's profits as a guideline, he estimated what they could expect to take in if they worked the land themselves for the next two years, and he jotted down the figure.

He didn't go out to his fields the next day. He puttered around the house, waiting.

Before long the black car of the previous day pulled off the highway and rolled to a stop in the driveway. This time two men climbed out.

The first man repeated his proposition and Mark confirmed some interest on the Hardmans' part. They got down to facts and figures.

How much would the Hardmans want in order to seal the deal?

How much would the company be willing to offer?

They jousted verbally, like two amiable boxers circling for an opening.

Then the stranger mentioned a figure. *The* figure. The same amount—*to the penny*—as the one Mark had decided on the night before. Now the Hardmans could turn all their attention to the Lord's work without losing a cent.

There was more. The company maintained a small house down the road. The Hardmans were welcome to live there, rent free, for the duration of the two-year lease.

In Book of Mormon times the brother of Jared saw the finger of the Lord touching stones to light his way.

The Hardmans believe his finger beckoned them, also, indicating clearly which road he desired them to follow. At the conclusion of their full-time stake labors, they were satisfied they had chosen well.

This faithful couple who originally worried about their ability to touch one investigator's heart had touched—and baptized—a grand total of *sixty-four* grateful fellow travelers they met along the way.

3
War and the
Hand of Destiny

Judy Allebes leaned her head back against the cushions of the luxurious airliner and closed her eyes. She was going home. It was 1982. More than forty years had come and gone, yet she could hear the metallic ring of hobnailed boots marching down the cobblestones of her native Holland and she could picture every detail of that invasion as clearly as if it were yesterday . . .

The brave soldiers of Holland fought savagely for five days trying to repulse the battalions of Nazis sweeping across their eastern border. It was a lost cause from the beginning.

Their numbers were mere handfuls compared to the endless hordes breaking through like waves dashing themselves onto the shore, human waves that were as impossible to turn aside.

After five days Queen Wilhelmina ordered her men to put up their guns. Resistance was useless.

It's difficult to comprehend the number of lives taken in that short period of time. It was May, 1940. The valiant dead were buried in mass graves, and the next May poppies sprang up volunteer to cover their graves—not familiar orange-colored poppies, but blossoms of a flaming, blood-red hue. Nobody could explain how that happened, but the living accepted the unusual flowers as a tribute to their noble dead.

The attack came as a surprise. Hitler, speaking to his countrymen, promised over and over that he would not allow Holland to be harmed. The Dutch were his friends, he said. Hadn't they welcomed German *Kinder* into their homes after World War I, to feed and nourish the little ones when all of Germany was starving?

Dutch citizens gathered around their radios to listen to Hitler's ravings. The hysterical quality of his voice made them uneasy, as did the thunderous responses of *Sieg Heil!* bursting from the throats of tens of thousands of his dedicated followers, but they tried hard to believe what he said.

Bombs rained on Holland for the first time on May 5, and in short order the cities of Rotterdam and Arnhem were flattened. Enemy bombers were probably already in the air while the Dutch prime minister's words on the radio assured his people they had nothing to fear because Hitler had pledged there would be no attack.

The comfortable Allebes home was one of the first houses to be confiscated. It stood in the village of Zandwoort, a beach resort on the shores of the North Sea, the point of land offering the most direct access to England. Some Nazi soldiers were under the delusion that a connecting bridge linked England and Holland together and that it originated in Zandwoort. Of course, there was no such bridge.

Judy, her husband, Ted, and their twelve-year-old son named after his father were infinitely more fortunate than their Jewish neighbors, who were rounded up and shipped via truck or cattlecar to Amsterdam and from there to concentration camps, carting with them only what they could cram into one suitcase. At least Judy and her family were permitted to keep their belongings. And none of their Jewish friends ever came back.

The printing plant where Ted worked was taken over by the Germans, cutting off his income. Overnight they were displaced from their home and Ted's livelihood. But they came from large, close-knit families in Haarlem to the north. They were lucky. They had someplace to go. They settled in with Judy's sister and stored their furniture in her mother-in-law's attic.

Judy sat up late one night in Haarlem, sewing name tags into every article of her husband's clothing. Her customarily neat stitches were a little ragged because tears made it difficult to see. The invaders had left them homeless; now they had sent notice that they also wanted her husband.

The orderly system of Dutch record keeping made it child's play to compile names and addresses of ablebodied men between the ages of eighteen and forty-five. Germany needed slave labor to till their fields and work in factories.

Ted was ablebodied and he was thirty-two years old. He was scheduled for pickup early the next morning, soon after the rising of the sun.

All night Judy sewed and prayed. She wasn't sure what she expected from the Lord, but she prayed hour after long hour that *something* would interfere with the kidnap of her husband.

At dawn word came through the grapevine—the office housing Ted's records had burned to the ground during the night. Sabotage, surely, but to Judy's thinking that made it no less her Heavenly Father's efficient answer to her prayers.

She was the only Latter-day Saint in her family at that time. The branch in Haarlem was small and the members widely scattered. Electricity and gas were cut off countrywide, and without heat or petrol to travel, there could be no meetings.

Life became increasingly harder to cope with. Cooking was done over a large paint can with holes drilled in the sides for ventilation. A small floor was fashioned halfway up the can, below which bits of wood and paper were stuffed and burned to furnish a modicum of heat. A cooking pot covered the top opening. They called it their emergency stove.

Judy desperately missed the companionship of other Saints in those trying times. But she knew the Lord had not forsaken the family. By some miracle her husband was with her still. That bolstered her courage enormously and gave her faith that they would be protected.

But Ted was never out of danger. The little family of three changed their residence often. Remaining in one spot was risky.

Shortly thereafter they took refuge with an elderly aunt, Tante Dora. Ted brought a few guilders into the household with his talent as an artist. He enlarged old photos, touched them up, and turned them into beautiful portraits.

The family found that the proverbial ill wind that blows good luck along with the bad now put food—of sorts—on the Allebes table. Nearly every Haarlem family grieved for a lost son blown away in the early days of the war, and sorrowing parents sought the mementos Ted created. They paid him what little they could spare, and it helped.

A system of austere rationing made food available to buy in sufficient quantity to sustain life, but just barely. Rations obtained with coupons brought in small amounts of food, but it was all of substitute quality and poor in nutritional value. War and hunger stalked the land hand in hand like two monstrous twins.

Ted and his son gathered dandelion greens from the fields to supplement what they were able to purchase, and they also tried out other weeds thought to be tolerable for human consumption. Their aim was to stay alive. They didn't haggle over the taste.

For grown men to appear openly on the streets was a situation fraught with danger. Even so, Ted took the family's coffee coupons to farmers from time to time to trade for a few morsels of precious, nourishing food. His bicycle tires disintegrated, and since there were no replacements, he bounced along clumsily on the bare rims.

They moved to the house of Judy's brother on the outskirts of town. Holland is a flat country. The brother's windows looked out across miles of beautiful green fields intersected by water canals and dotted with whirling windmills. Now they were closer to farmlands and it was easier for Ted to slip out to forage for something they could eat.

One morning, very early, he pedaled his bike along the bumpy country road. Unexpectedly a brand new wall slowed his progress. Armed troopers waited at the other side of the small gateway to pounce on unwary travelers, and with four or five other passersby Ted was caught as neatly as an unsuspecting mosquito in the sticky web of a black widow spider.

Bicycles and identification cards were snatched out of their hands and the shaken prisoners were shoved into a circle. A guard carrying a loaded rifle paced back and forth, back and forth, to keep them in line against the new wall.

They would be shipped off to Germany as soon as the quota was filled, and their wives would be left behind to weep at their unexplained disappearance.

Suddenly, out of the corner of his eye, Ted caught sight of a young girl standing apart in the shadows. Each time the guard turned his back, she bravely whispered encouragement. She spoke so softly he wasn't certain she really spoke. "Can I do something for you? Should I notify your family?"

Ted watched his chance and whispered back. His confiscated I.D. card still bore their former address at Judy's aunt's, but in reality they'd lived with her brother for almost a week. He softly repeated the brother's street and house number.

He was heartsick, anticipating the grief Judy would endure at his loss. He wanted to spare her the added pain of listening for his footsteps or constantly hoping against hope that he might return. The going would be a little easier if she knew what had happened to him.

A speeding truck interrupted their whispers. In a desperate bid to pull out of the trap, the driver hurtled his vehicle through the gate without stopping, but soldiers leaped to their motorcycles and roared off in wild pursuit.

Their own guard was momentarily distracted and he, too, ran a few steps in the speeding truck's direction.

Ted was the only prisoner with enough presence of mind to run. The others were too frightened. He took off across the fields like a shot, crouching low, turning frantically down the first street he came to.

Knocking on a strange door could be as dangerous in those days as staying at the wall would have been. There was no sure method to predict who lived inside – whether the knock and plea for help would be answered by a loyal patriot or by one who had sold out to the enemy in return for special privileges. But there was no alternative.

Ted banged loudly on the first door he reached, and once again, mercifully, a protecting hand hovered over him. He was quickly drawn inside, then hidden there until after dark. His hospitable host scraped together a few ingredients and brewed a bowl of thin soup, which he graciously shared with Ted.

Meanwhile, the brave girl in the shadows was true to her promise. She contacted Judy without delay and related the whole story of capture and escape.

Persons living cat-and-mouse lives learn to think quickly. Judy's sharpened wits immediately sensed another danger. Tante Dora lived all the way across town, and she must be warned not to divulge their whereabouts. The question was, How could they reach her in time?

Young Ted ran like the wind. Mile after mile he flew, never stopping to catch his breath or to ease the knifelike pain that stabbed at his side. He couldn't stop; his father's life was at stake.

He staggered up Tante Dora's steps and delivered his message, but he was none too soon. Uniformed officers pulled up to the curb as he slipped back down off the porch and melted into the shadows.

If they intended to frighten her into talking, they reckoned without the courage of Tante Dora. She was elderly, but she had more than her quota of spunk. Feisty by nature, she was not one to be ordered about by anyone.

Nobody by the name of Allebes lived in her house! Her name was Vlaming. She invited them in to look around.

Perhaps she enjoyed outwitting the cocky young upstarts who dared to question her word. If so, her enjoyment cooled after a few of their famous, surprise, midnight raids. Eventually they gave up trying to make her talk and they left her in peace.

Ted, Jr., was not old enough to be considered of value to the Nazi troops and he moved about the streets freely. He was of great value to Ted and Judy. He acted as the family eyes and ears, their private alarm system.

His warning salvaged their warm blankets. His news of trucks moving through the neighborhood picking up armloads of thick, woolen bedding, for which Holland was famous, gave them time to strip the beds, hide the good blankets in a crawlway under the house next to the water pipes, and remake the beds with old ones.

Judy needed her blankets. She didn't object to giving up the older ones, but as it turned out the looters didn't want *them* either.

Young Ted's next warning was much more chilling. This time it wasn't blankets the *Wehrmacht* sought. They were stopping at each house to drag out extra slaves for the Fatherland, and they were almost at the door.

Ted and Piet, Judy's brother, were making candles in the living room, and wax and wicks were heaped on the table before them. There was no time to put them away.

They leaped to their feet and bolted up the steep, narrow stairs two at a time with Judy following. Young Ted took over their place at the table.

They continued upwards until they reached the walk-in closet off the third-story bedroom. Dislodging a loose panel at the closet's rear wall, the two men wiggled through the opening.

A brick chimney filled the space behind the closet. By standing erect and hugging the bricks, two grown men could disappear into what appeared to be no empty space at all.

Judy rearranged the loosened panel behind them and quickly looked around. Fervently she prayed that no incriminating detail had been overlooked in their haste. Then she raced feverishly back down the stairs.

She forced her rapid breathing to subside and hoped she and her son could present a picture of calm tranquility, though inwardly they seethed with fear. Then she answered the knock on the door.

Everything of material worth in their home had already been traded for food. Carpets had long since vanished, and Judy cringed as two pairs of boots with protruding nails tramped roughly across her bare wooden floors.

The boots paused briefly while their owners inspected the inexperienced fumblings of the boy at the table. "That's not the way it's done," they laughed mockingly; and, delighted at the chance to exhibit superior knowledge, they offered him a few pointers on candlemaking. The boy thanked them most politely.

Then they got down to serious business. Where was the father of the house?

Their search started on the ground floor and continued through the second and third floors until they reached the bedroom and stepped into the closet. Judy's heart hammered so loudly in her chest she couldn't believe they didn't hear it.

In flashback she saw herself watching a movie newsreel, gasping in horror at atrocities of the Spanish civil war some years before. She heard herself cry out to her husband, "How can people live like that?"

Now she understood how the Spanish citizens had managed. When the lives of loved ones hang in the balance, one remains calm and does what one must.

But oh, how she prayed! The chimney was dusty. One cough or sneeze and every member of the household would be gunned down on the spot.

The soldiers inspected clothes hanging within inches of the loosened panel. They lingered as if they suspected, like children playing an innocent game of hide and seek, that they were getting warmer. Warm, but never hot, and they left the house emptyhanded.

From then on, Ted and Piet didn't risk showing themselves on the streets. Young Ted took over as provider, and under his father's tutelage he traded or scrounged what they required to stay alive.

The war ended, finally, in 1945. Planes flying low overhead during the endless years of occupation had produced terror in Dutch hearts. Now the whir of engines sounded like music when they knew the planes flew from Canada with lifegiving packages of food aboard. Crackers, dried milk, dried eggs, cereal—anything that didn't break on impact or require refrigeration was dropped, and it fell like manna from heaven.

Latter-day Saint missionaries returned to the country and Church meetings were resumed. Judy was called to preside over the Primary in the branch. She and the missionaries ran it alone. No member sisters lived close enough to help in the middle of the week.

A manual of lessons arrived from Salt Lake City, and while he was assigned to the area one Elder played the piano. Soon three member children and twenty-seven others attended regularly, and they presented a touching Mother's Day program. Following that experience several parents began to accompany their boys or girls to Sunday School.

During the bleak war years Judy had been sustained by the belief that the family's destiny would take them to America to mingle with the body of the Saints. Ted was baptized after fighting stopped, and that certainly helped, but she had a tremendous desire to live surrounded by people who believed as she did.

But emigrating required money. Judy wasn't trained in a moneymaking craft. Ted returned to the printing plant, but every cent of his salary was needed for their living expenses.

Once again help came when it was needed. While they waited for their official travel application to rise to the top of the list, a friend in the ice cream business hired Judy to dip vanilla bars into chocolate topping and he agreed to lend them the portion of the needed amount not covered by her wages.

She knew in her heart that the move was right for them, but when the magic moment came she was desolate at leaving the Primary children without spiritual guidance. She simply couldn't go and desert them.

Her best friend, Ans Okker, lived around the corner. She was indignant. "Don't you dare pass up this opportunity! You've waited so long. I don't belong to your church, but my children enjoy your Primary. Before I'd let you stay home, I'd take it over myself!"

Ans proved to be the perfect replacement, and Judy was free to go with a happy heart. Ans was dependable; she diligently studied the manual from cover to cover; *and* — she played the piano!

Judy opened her eyes and smiled at her reflection. She leaned to peer out of the window as her plane circled Amsterdam.

Looking back over the rough seas of her life, she recognized that her family had passed through some pretty frightening times, but by holding fast to the hand of the Lord they had weathered the storms. They had been led to safety in a port where it felt right for them to be.

Ted's testimony had flourished in Utah and California. Young Ted, who was baptized in America, had grown strong in the gospel and married a fine woman there, and their three beautiful daughters embodied all the traits Judy could have wished for in her grandchildren.

Her smile deepened. God was no respecter of persons. Even as he guided and protected them, he was gently leading her dear friend toward a beautiful, new life. Two months after her kindness in releasing Judy to leave Holland, Ans had been baptized. Like ripples in a stream, the effects of her good deed had broadened to touch many lives and had brought new purpose into her own.

Now, forty years later, this wonderful trip was a gift to Judy from Ans and her husband, a tangible token of thanks for the destiny that had helped to shape both of their lives.

4
A Message
From the Sea

"Do you still have it with you? May we see it, please?"

Aleida went to a cabinet and brought her treasure to us, carrying it reverently as befits a pearl of great price.

It didn't *look* valuable, covered as it was with plain, ordinary brown wrapping paper. She bent to lower it into my hands as my husband and I waited on the leather couch in her home.

We had driven seventy-five miles, and if the experience we expected to hear in detail that morning fulfilled its promise, this item would be one of the most unusual religious objects I had ever touched.

At first the island of Biak in the South Pacific was a literal paradise to the Hermann family after the terrible years of World War II.

Aleida and René were married in 1946. They moved to the island, to a house on the beach where white sands dipped to the sea and clear water sparkled over colored coral on the ocean's floor.

Swimming and boating filled their days. Being in a world at peace was, of course, a great relief. Surrounded by palm trees swaying overhead and other lush vegetation between the water's edge and the jungle, they feasted on bananas and picked coconuts from their own trees. They had come from the city, but initially they enjoyed the isolation and the primitive surroundings.

Aleida was born in Sumatra to an Indonesian/Portuguese mother and a Dutch physician father. For twenty-four years her life was comfortable, with servants on hand to attend to her needs.

Then, with a rude shock, she was jolted from her naive childhood dreams.

She followed in the medical footsteps of her father and enrolled in nurses training on the island of Java. The pitiful condition of her patients brought her face to face with the harsh realities of life as an angel of mercy.

She hated nursing in those days, and often she cried herself to sleep at night, the pillow soaked with her tears.

She forced herself to adjust to her duties and thought she had become conditioned to human misery. She nursed patients who had frightful tropical diseases. The hardest cases were the children, isolated in tiny glass rooms because of their terrible contagion.

Then, at the end of her third year, the war raged. Japan invaded Java and took over the hospital.

We'll glide over the long, nerve-shattering war years. Aleida was strong and she seemed to cope fairly well with that experience.

The war was over when she married René Hermann, a Dutch survivor of enemy concentration camps and a man who also had painful memories he was trying to forget. He was employed by the Dutch government as a building construction supervisor. His new assignment took them to Biak in Dutch New Guinea, off the northern tip of Australia.

Biak was a natural paradise. It was also a key position during South Pacific struggles for supremacy between Japanese and American troops. The soldiers were gone when the Hermanns arrived, but their implements of destruction were left behind to scar the peace of the landscape.

Aleida tried to ignore disabled American planes that dotted the green hillsides while they waited silently to be dismantled by work crews.

She tried to shut her ears to ghostly screams that still seemed to ring from a local cave, from the throats of fifty Japanese who chose cremation by flamethrower rather than leave the cave and surrender to their enemies.

And her movements about the island were somewhat restricted. Papuan natives of Biak were more civilized than the fierce headhunters of the Manus culture on New Guinea, but their veneer of civilization was at best thin. She heard grisly tales of ears brutally hacked from heads of soldiers during the war.

Echoes of death and destruction haunted her daily and stirred sleeping memories she had hoped to be able to suppress.

Five babies joined the family in rapid succession, and their mother worried about their future. What chance did children have in a world which would permit such unspeakable atrocities?

She sank into a depression that deepened steadily. Worst of all, her lifelong belief in a supreme being, a belief that had sustained her like a candle flame of hope, flickered and appeared to approach extinction. She mourned its loss as she might agonize at the death of a dear, departed friend.

The Bible, once an important source of her strength, lost its meaning. She thought, "That was a story for my grandmother. It has nothing to do with the times I live in."

She pondered intensely on the meaning of life. Her questions went unanswered, questions of importance to her troubled soul. In all good conscience she could not pass on a sustaining faith to her children, and she was filled with per-

vading sadness at this. She feared she had lost her belief in
God.

But faith as vigorous as Aleida's once was doesn't give up
without a mighty struggle to survive, and she tried once more.
"Heavenly Father, I need so *desperately* to know you are
there. If you do exist, please—please let me know."

She doesn't remember exactly how many days it took to
receive her answer. Probably a week or two. Certainly not
longer than a month.

A friend occupied a small cabin directly behind her
family's. He wasn't well educated, but he owned a modest
library and she was looking for something to read.

He offered a book she might be interested in. It resembled
the Bible in some respects but was different. He couldn't
identify it because the front cover and title pages were missing.

The fascinating part of the story was how it came to be in
his possession. He found it. As he stood in the harbor, it
floated toward him across the ocean, alone, riding the waves in
solitary splendor.

A native helper swam out to retrieve it for him and plucked
it—dripping—from the surface of the sea.

His eyes scanned the empty horizon. There were no ships of
any variety in sight.

The book must have bobbed up and down in the water for
hours or even days, but surprisingly, when he opened it the
pages were dry! How that could happen he was at a loss to
explain. But it was printed in Dutch, and Aleida was welcome
to borrow it.

She eagerly accepted his offer and hurried to her home.
Once she began reading it, she couldn't put the book down.
Her husband shared her elation, and together they devoured it
from beginning to end.

Testimonies preceded the main narrative—witnesses to the
truthfulness of the manuscript. Reference was made to some
miraculous means by which the record came to be. The testimonies made a lasting impression on the Hermanns.

They read it all and found only truth. The problem was that after closing the final page there was nowhere else for them to go. There was no clue as to where the book came from. They firmly believed that the Lord had sent his answer to their prayers, but what did he expect them to do next?

A few days later Aleida opened a letter from her mother in Holland and read: "Aleida, I was shopping in The Hague yesterday and happened to run across a friend of yours from the past. I enclose her address in case you'd care to contact her."

Aleida was overjoyed. That woman was one of the best friends she'd ever had, her roommate at a convent boarding school, but they had lost contact.

In her first communication to her old friend she quoted phrases from the new book, the book that belonged to her now, since she had traded an enormous salmon-like fish to her neighbor in return for the privilege of keeping it forever.

The answer to all her questions came by return mail. "Where did you get a copy of the Book of Mormon? There are no missionaries in your part of the world and yet I recognize your quotations. I'm curious, because I have just joined the Mormon Church."

I gently lifted the brown paper, cut to size to protect the object I held in my hands, and examined the book that had altered Aleida's life and the lives of her husband and children.

She had begged for a message from the Lord and she had been true to its coming. She and René sold all they owned and moved to Holland, where they applied for baptism. The impossible difficulty of that move is a story in itself that deserves someday to be told. Hearing it impressed on my mind how sincerely the Hermanns accepted this book as an answer from the Lord, but I wanted to decide for myself.

The back cover and binding were still firmly attached, but they were badly warped—bubbled here, shrunken there, as one would expect from a book fished out of the sea. That was understandable.

What was almost unbelievable—but undeniably true—was the mint condition of the text. The pages should have been as warped as the cover—maybe more so, because the paper is more delicate. But they lay flat and unblemished as if they were newly printed. Even the edges were free from stain. The printing was clear and unsmudged. The only restriction barring me from reading each word on every page was my unfamiliarity with Dutch.

But the book wasn't meant for me. It had been sent to Aleida. It was only a means to an end, of course, but the fact that it was printed in Dutch, plus suspension of the normal functioning of the elements while it floated in the water, combined to reinforce to my mind what the Hermanns believe.

I could think of only one explanation: It must have been vitally important to the God Aleida couldn't bear to give up that she read that particular message.

5
The Devil's Grip

Learning to live by the Spirit in times of serenity comes in handy when the going gets rough.

Elder Matt Drumright had been at the Missionary Training Center in Provo, Utah, for only two weeks when he suspected something might be seriously wrong. Purple spots up and down his legs were the first indication.

His spots might have been overlooked in the absence of other, more noticeable symptoms, except that he had seen purple spots once before.

Blotches on his little sister's body years earlier turned out to be warning signals of a rare blood disorder. After specialized treatment her condition cleared, but she still went in for periodic checkups. Much as he hated to admit it, Matt knew instinctively that he needed the services of a physician.

Actually, there *were* other symptoms. He had a fever and felt unnaturally tired, and once or twice his nose had bled in the shower, but those were minor inconveniences, explained away as reactions to yellow fever and typhoid shots administered at the MTC. The shots, plus the vigorous 6:00 A.M. to 10:30 P.M. study schedule, could easily produce fatigue.

His mission call was to Bolivia/Santa Cruz, and he was excited. He needed long hours of study—and the shots—to become the missionary he'd worked toward being all the years of his life. His shaky high school Spanish needed all the help it could get.

As long as he could remember he'd prepared for that moment. Pennies presented to him as a baby were deposited by his mother and dad into a special mission account. Later he took over the fund on his own. At thirteen and fourteen, after tithing payments practically every cent he earned from a paper route went into the bank. One summer his blossoming account expanded through his hard work on a farm in Idaho.

Now he had embarked on the long-awaited adventure, was living the dream he'd looked forward to with years of eager anticipation. It was annoying to find those spots and be forced to interrupt his busy schedule to visit a doctor. But he did go.

The doctor performed a series of blood tests, then invited him into the office. Keeping their discussion deliberately low-key, he talked Matt into going home for a while. More tests were needed and they should be done at home.

Matt didn't want to leave but there was no choice. The doctor called the mission president and a reluctant young Elder flew home on the very next plane.

He hadn't heard how plainly the doctor laid out the problem to his shocked parents on the telephone. Their son's white blood count was dangerously elevated with the white cells abnormal, and his platelet count was extremely low. Something *was* seriously wrong. It could be leukemia. Did they know a good hematologist who specialized also in oncology, or the treatment of various forms of cancer?

They did. Their daughter's checkups were handled by that type of specialist and they had confidence in his ability.

The wheels of Matt's plane touched down at midnight. By nine o'clock the next morning he sat in the hospital watching warily as more blood flowed out of his arm into a laboratory technician's test tubes.

The kindly doctor was obviously moved when he spoke to Jim and Marilyn Drumright that afternoon. Their son did have leukemia, and it didn't look promising. He had to admit that at that time up to 95 percent of the victims of that particular form of the disease did not survive.

Matt's parents were strong. The thought occurred to them that those negative statistics turned around meant that 5 percent did survive, and they determined that their son would be one of the fortunate few.

The next day the doctor sat on the edge of the hospital bed. He is personable, a man Matt's sister affectionately calls her "mad scientist."

He laid one hand gently on his youthful patient's shoulder and said, "Well, we have a challenge ahead of us—a big one. I'm afraid you have leukemia."

He didn't mention the types of treatment Matt would have to undergo, or bring up possible side effects. He didn't speak of painful spinal taps, nor of the three varieties of drugs given in doses massive enough to kill off abnormal cells but held barely short of being fatal to the patient.

Radiation and chemotherapy—and falling hair—were not discussed at that time. Better cross one hurdle at a time.

Matt might not have been familiar with details, but he knew enough about radiation and chemotherapy and their effects generally to be certain that what lay ahead would take all the strength he could muster. But his reply was, "How soon can we lick this challenge so I can get back to work?"

He wasn't really frightened for the loss of his life. He felt a calmness which assured him that in spite of everything he faced, all would eventually be well.

He remembered the words of his college institute director: "It doesn't really matter what happens—to us or in the world around us. All we have to worry about is doing right things. If we do, the Lord will bless us. Whatever befalls us along the way will be only a setback, nothing more." Matt's dominant characteristic has always been a desire to serve the Lord, and that desire had not weakened.

The treatment *was* far from pleasant. After a week or so he was allowed to go home on an out-patient basis.

But at home or in the hospital, he considered himself a missionary and he acted accordingly. As a matter of fact, the entire Drumright family adopted missionary standards.

Honoring his urgent request, mission leaders agreed not to release him. Instead he was given a medical leave. To Elder Drumright this "setback" was temporary, and the minutes or hours he could snatch between bouts of nausea or pain too intense for concentration, he devoted to scripture study or worked on perfecting his rusty Spanish.

Mission rules don't allow for listening to radios or watching TV, and Elder Drumright wanted to abide by the rules. Family members went along with him and didn't complain. They look back on that difficult period as one of special closeness—to each other and to the Lord.

Tapes of inspirational messages by Church authorities were played by the hour. Long, intimate talks cemented new closeness. He was always a self-sufficient child and young man, but he learned to rely on the help of others as his condition worsened and he couldn't help himself. He felt new gratitude for his parents' love and learned compassion toward anyone who suffered an affliction of any kind. His empathy for the willing sacrifices of the Savior increased many-fold.

He'd been given a blessing at the training center, then another at home from his father and the stake president. Additional spiritual help came from every direction. Members of the ward organized and set aside a day of fasting and prayer. A friend kept his name on the prayer list of the temple.

His stake president sympathized with the difficulty of studying a foreign language alone in his condition and issued a formal call to a recently returned missionary from a Spanish-speaking area. When Matt was up to it, they studied together.

Last but by no means least, the Drumrights took comfort in knowing that, as a missionary in need, his plight held the attention of the prophet and the other apostles, who weekly petitioned the Lord in Elder Drumright's behalf. The household radiated with determined optimism.

Nevertheless, despite optimism and powerful prayers, Matt's ordeal grew harder to bear. Leukemia wasn't his only battleground. Strange and unusual ailments popped up regularly. A lump appeared on the middle of his back and increased to half the size of a grapefruit before it disappeared.

Part of the time he walked with what his parents called "the low ceiling effect," with head bent parallel to the floor. Raising it to an upright position brought on excruciating headaches once the spinal taps were begun.

For a while he walked with a decided limp; next he couldn't walk at all. By then the slightest movement of his bed or a gentle touch from his mother when she attended to his needs caused extreme discomfort.

Almost total paralysis set in. He could move his hands, slowly and with great difficulty, turn his neck, and wiggle his toes. Those feeble movements were all that stood between him and complete immobility, and his pain was impossible to describe.

Marilyn and Jim slept fitfully at night and then only because of a smoke alarm positioned an inch or two away from Matt's fingers. If he woke and needed help, he could inch his hand over to touch the alarm button and rouse them.

He felt as he supposed it must feel to be very, very old. Stages resembling rapid aging reduced him in a few short weeks from a healthy, vigorous missionary to a paralyzed, pain-wracked shell. Memory faltered and concentration was next to impossible. The only strong thing remaining was his dogged determination not to give up.

Even his doctor was puzzled at his condition. Some of the advanced symptoms didn't fit the pattern of leukemia. Something else had to be at work there.

Tests showed that the weakened body had been attacked fiercely by a virus so rare that Matt's doctor had never seen a case of it. Medical specialists were at a loss to explain its presence in his system.

The insidious ailment had attacked the muscles to cause paralysis. A biopsy on one of the arm muscles was scheduled as a starting point. Perhaps that would furnish some clue to the nature of the disease and its possible treatment.

Ordinarily biopsies are not particularly dangerous and often are performed in a chair in the doctor's office. In view of Matt's frail condition, however, they couldn't afford to take chances, so the operating room was booked. It would be a serious procedure.

He was readmitted on the day previously set aside by his ward for fasting and prayer. It was Sunday, and several hundred friends spent a good portion of that Sabbath pleading for his life.

Two days later Marilyn reached the hospital room at 7:00 A.M., shaky, prepared to wait out the dreaded surgery. Instead, she was greeted by radiant nurses, a beaming doctor, and a grateful son. The virus's hold had loosened unexpectedly and surgery would not be necessary after all.

That was the turning point. The virus continued to recede and Matt's leukemia began to respond to chemotherapy.

Four months after a dejected Elder flew home to an uncertain prognosis, he made a triumphant—if weak—return. He wasn't well. His leukemia was in remission and he was fighting for strength. The medication's side effects had drained him tremendously and he needed time to recover.

Before leaving home he slept an average of fourteen hours a night and napped during the daytime. He worried about how his body would respond to the demands of the long MTC hours, but he agitated for permission to go back.

At first his doctor wasn't enthusiastic about the move. He reserved the right to approve or reject the new calling's location. It had to be somewhere in the United States and near a city large enough to hold a competent specialist, because to keep the leukemia in remission chemotherapy would be continued weekly without interruption.

Elder Drumright's stake president personally took the case to the Missionary Committee in Salt Lake City, and it was decided to assign Matt to the Florida/Fort Lauderdale Mission, laboring among Spanish-speaking investigators. The doctor agreed.

The missionary joined a class already in progress at the MTC and pampered himself to the extent of sleeping half an hour beyond the customary six o'clock morning wake-up call, and of napping for forty-five minutes during P.E. period. Otherwise, though it sounds unusual in describing a missionary, he functioned as one of the "regular guys."

With one exception. Matt continually pushed falling strands of hair off his books and gathered them into little piles.

Two days before leaving for Florida, he stared at himself in the mirror and a shiny scalp gleamed back. He had two choices: He could present himself in Fort Lauderdale as bald as Yul Brynner or he could resort to the indignity of a wig. The wig was the lesser of two evils.

He bought a hairpiece remarkably like his own hair and had it trimmed. It was close to missionary standards, but not quite. Further snipping would expose the wig's backing, so it would have to do.

Elder Drumright went to Florida and filled an honorable mission. His efforts to perform to his own satisfaction took more courage than many of us would be able to sustain. The going was rough, but he never lost his sense of humor. More than one new companion needled him about the length of his hair and was startled when his answer was to reach up and remove it altogether.

Matt is a private, modest person. He doesn't complain and he doesn't speak openly about the successes I hear about from another source.

He will say that there were times when, as with other

Elders, he knew that his placement in that particular mission had surely been dictated by the Lord. He is convinced he was a specific person in a specific place at a specified time, filling needs that were unique to his special abilities and talents.

The day came when a little fuzz grew back on his head and he could say, "When Wiggy goes, wiggy goes." His current companion's nickname was Wiggy, and he was due to be released. When Wiggy boarded the plane, Elder Drumright removed his wig permanently, boxed it up, and shipped it home. Hair five-eighths of an inch long was long enough! That's typical of how his problems were handled.

Today, as I write, Matt is the picture of good health. Thirty months of chemotherapy—taken orally during the last few months—have ended.

This story wouldn't be complete without one final addition.

When Matt lay in the hospital in his home town and the mysterious ailment just as mysteriously gave way, Marilyn pressed the doctor for specific information. What was the virus, exactly? Did it have a name?

The doctor smiled grimly. He replied, "You'll never believe it when I tell you. It has a long scientific identity, but the name it goes by is *the Devil's Grip.*

The Drumrights and their friends weren't too surprised. All along they'd strongly suspected that the devil was somehow involved.

6
The Last Race

It was Saturday afternoon, June 7, 1980, the first sunny day of the season. After an unusually long, cold winter, the air was still chilled and the warm sun felt heavenly as it ricocheted off the water onto their faces.

Utah Lake is always cold. It sits west of Mount Timpanogos outside of Provo, Utah. Its boundaries measure twenty-three miles by eight miles, figuring out to be one hundred and fifty square miles of icy water fed by melting snow flowing down from the mountain's summit. Even in the heat of summer the peaks are capped with snow.

Kathie and Karl were water skiing on Utah Lake that afternoon. Actually, Karl and his former missionary companion were skiing; Kathie rested quietly in the boat enjoying the sunshine, although probably she shouldn't have been there.

Her first child was only two weeks old and she was supposed to be taking it easy. The birth had been difficult and involved considerable tearing, and she would require an extended period for recuperation.

But two weeks of confinement is a long siege for a lively temperament and she needed a change. She would be careful not to overdo. The baby was left with a trusted neighbor and the mother would be back before the next scheduled feeding.

Half sitting, half lying in the boat, Kathie daydreamed about how she and her husband had happened to meet, and how strange are the roles of coincidence in our lives. She enrolled at Brigham Young University after completion of a mission in Spain. On the campus grounds one morning she crossed paths with her former mission zone leader. He asked her out. They dated and fell in love; married; and ultimately little Bonnie was born.

Her mother and father were delighted with Kathie's choice and so were we. She had spent her teenage years in our home ward. Karl has a close relationship with the Lord, so her parents were happy to entrust their daughter's well-being to his care.

But lately Karl hadn't felt up to par. Physical exertion brought on spells of weakness bordering at times on temporary paralysis.

Eating at frequent intervals seemed to help, but he couldn't figure out why. He hadn't then received results of medical tests which would pinpoint the cause of the weakness as hypoglycemia, a bloodstream sugar deficiency opposite to diabetes.

Hypoglycemia is regulated by diet and small snacks at frequent intervals, but he didn't know that. In order to be controlled, the affliction first must be identified.

Feeling as he did, if he hadn't understood Kathie's real need for a change he wouldn't have consented to go on this outing.

Karl and Jim skiied vigorously for two hours before Karl began to seriously tire. He hadn't packed a snack to munch on, so between lack of food and fatigue from exertion he'd definitely had his full quota of exercise for one day. It was time to head for home.

Their decision to go was made in the middle of the lake with miles of water separating them from land. But then a shear pin snapped on the motor's propeller. The damage wasn't crucial because they carried spare parts, and replacing the broken pin was a fairly simple procedure.

Karl and his friend hoisted the engine inside and bent over it while Kathie watched from the other end. At that moment, the violent storm struck with fury.

Without warning, a howling wind whipped over the crest of Mount Timpanogos. In line with the configuration of the mountain in juxtaposition with the lake, the wind plummeted down from the peaks and hit the lake like a projectile shot out of a cannon. Bouncing back upwards, it scooped tons of water into frightening waves that broke over their heads.

Other small crafts dotted the vicinity, but at the first sign of trouble they scattered. Sudden storms are not uncommon on Utah Lake, and experienced skippers wisely headed for shore without delay. Only one boat was in a disabled condition and could not run from the gale.

The two men worked quickly. They were almost finished with the repairs when a particularly gusty blast plumped up a giant wave as if it were a pillow in a pillow fight and tossed it in their direction. The boat was swamped. It shuddered and flipped end over end, flinging them headlong into the icy water with no protection other than life jackets. And then it sank.

Jackets may keep swimmers afloat in calm seas, but they are useless to hold heads free in a storm as violent as the one the three were now forced to battle. Water crashed over and around them and pushed them deep beneath the surface. They fought their way up to the top to fill bursting lungs with one quick gulp of air, only to have the next wave break over them, and the next, and the next.

Jim is a strong swimmer. Had he struck out for shore immediately, he might have made it. But he didn't even consider that course of action. He wouldn't leave his friends.

They fought the rampaging elements together for fully an

hour and a half. They were numb from the cold, and Karl felt himself slipping into shock. Kathie noticed with alarm that his shouted comments of encouragement were becoming somewhat incoherent. On Karl's part, he agonized that lack of strength prevented him from actively helping his wife.

It grew dark and colder, but they hardly noticed. Bonnie was uppermost in their thoughts. It was inconceivable and absolutely unacceptable that their lives should end there on the lake. Not then! Not with tiny Bonnie's whole future ahead of her. There had to be a way to escape.

Jim mentioned it first. "Karl," he shouted hoarsely, "can't we use our priesthood to call for help?"

Prescribed priesthood ordinances, such as laying on of hands for the purpose of healing the sick, for example, are far removed from extricating three people from certain death in the middle of a freezing lake. Karl had no organized written precedent to guide him. And yet the priesthood he held was the power by which the heavens and the earth were created.

Karl shouted back, "Maybe so, when worse comes to worse. I'll think about it."

Jim slapped his fist against the water in frustration. "Buddy," he shrieked against the howling wind, "the worst is here! We're going under. Get on with it!"

His analysis of the situation was correct. They couldn't hang on much longer. They were three exhausted people battling cold and bone-wrenching weariness in the dark, miles from help, and they were losing the fight.

Karl raised his arm toward heaven in supplication. In a shaky voice, he invoked the power he held so dear. He pronounced a blessing on boats still anywhere on the lake, urged them to come to the rescue, and promised them safety from the ravaging storm.

Twenty minutes slipped by with no rescue in sight while they continued to flounder. For Kathie and Karl, it was impossible to keep up the struggle. They were tossed to and fro at the mercy of the merciless wind.

Jim recognized at that point that he *must* leave the others. His own strength was almost spent. If one of them sank he couldn't prevent it, and he had given up hope of being found where they were. Only a madman would venture onto the lake before morning, and by morning it would be too late. He struck off in the general direction of the shore.

Meanwhile, back at the dock two sailboats were tied up at anchor with sails furled and stored away, a time-consuming process. Their owners had a passion for racing, and on that day one had emerged from every race victorious, much to the chagrin of the loser. The storm cut their competition short, and their last sprint was to race the storm, itself, back to port. They were lucky to have made it.

The winner couldn't believe his ears when he heard his companion call out across the water, "Hey! How about one last try? I'll beat you this time—I know I can. How about it? Or are you afraid?"

He paused with his hand on the mast. That had to be the craziest, most insane challenge anyone had ever hurled his way. Go back out to the ferocity of the storm when they were snug and safe in the harbor? He couldn't be serious.

But he was, and he didn't give up. The challenges increased in intensity until they reached a point of personal honor, and finally the victor agreed. They pulled their rolled-up sails out of the storage compartments and prepared for one final, foolhardy race.

They passed Jim by in the darkness. They didn't see him, but because their boats were powered by wind rather than driven by motors, his frantic screams for help reached their ears. They scooped him out of the water and, following his directions, pushed ahead to rescue Karl and Kathie.

It wasn't a second too soon. Kathie was as limp as a drowned kitten and Karl's last conscious memory of that night is seeing the shadows of two boats loom out of the blackness. He slipped into total shock before they reached him.

He has no recollection of being fished from the water completely incoherent, nor of being wrapped in a spare sail and slipped into a storage bin as protection from added exposure.

He suffered from severe hypothermia, made considerably worse by his undiagnosed and untreated hypoglycemia.

Jim checked the time sequence once they were safely on board and headed for shore. It had been roughly half an hour since Karl beseeched the powers of heaven to act upon any boat close enough to come to their aid.

The two Samaritans of the sailboats didn't have access to that information. Not religiously inclined, they were still puzzled by their actions. Nothing in their backgrounds prepared them to consider themselves as answers to a prayer that defies logic.

Jim questioned the men. How much time had elapsed since their unreasonable urge to return to the lake to participate in one last, suicidal race?

He really didn't need to ask. Before they opened their mouths to answer, he knew exactly what they would say.

7
"Phil"

"When I check out, I won't leave alone! Two hundred to three hundred people will go with me. I want all of you down there to know that. One man I'll take with me is so prominent that headlines will scream his name from every front page in the country!"

During the year I had worked as a volunteer crisis counselor for the Suicide Prevention Agency, we'd received periodic phone calls from a male with a beautifully modulated, resonant voice. He was fortyish in age, well educated, wonderfully articulate – and deadly.

He claimed to be an expert shot with a rifle, and often his calmly stated intentions were accompanied by dull metallic clicks as the hammer of his gun slammed against a temporarily empty chamber, lending chilling emphasis to his words.

He was employed in some unstated capacity at a city hospital, and his co-workers had no inkling of the consuming rage festering inside of him with white-hot heat.

His messages were never long ones. He called to remind us that written journals and cassette recordings would be ready for publication after the grisly deed was done. He wanted the world to appreciate the superb intricacy of his planning and execution, and to understand what unhappy factors from his background had propelled him to his mass revenge.

On his first call, he pinpointed his exact target date. It was nearly a year away. During that year of waiting, I didn't happen to speak with him personally. None of his calls coincided with my working hours, for which I was immensely grateful, but his plans were the talk of the agency.

Knowing the specific, proposed date, I consulted my schedule and relaxed. Portions of our training had dealt with the art of expressing concern and feeling it, but not allowing ourselves to become immobilized by pity or fear. Efficiency in critical conversations hangs on ability to think clearly. Hopefully the sound of a calm, confident voice may swing the scales away from irrationality and back to sanity for a distraught caller who has lost control.

Besides, and more to the point, according to the schedule I wouldn't be anywhere near the premises that fateful day, so I could afford to relax.

One brisk fall morning I reached the agency suite at sunrise. I rapped on the windowpane of one of the conference rooms to alert the volunteer who had been on duty all night that his replacement had arrived and waited to be let in.

I asked the standard questions: "Has it been busy? Anything going on I should know about?"

He barked: "You're pretty calm! Don't you realize what day this is?"

I racked my brain. It was Monday, I knew that for sure, but what was the date? A few hasty calculations and it hit me right between the eyes: November 15. How could that be? I had checked the schedule carefully and my shift didn't fall even close to November 15. Had I neglected to check again after the schedules were changed? Apparently so.

By then I felt fairly confident in my work, as confident as one ever is in situations of life and death, but I certainly wasn't primed to handle this one. Facing the possibility that one person's life may stand or fall on a volunteer's ability to touch a responsive chord is one thing; setting myself up as the last human contact before a brilliant but violent man snuffed out innocent bystanders was more than I bargained for. I shivered, and it wasn't from the cold.

When Ted walked out of the door, I would be alone. Just me and the phones—with no doubt in my mind that "Phil"[1] would call before setting off on his errand of death. After a year of agency conversations, what could *I* possibly say at this final hour to deter him?

I tried to settle down in my lonely vigil. The phone's shrill ring startled me twice, but it was nothing serious. One pleasant male voice asked how to go about volunteering. I directed him to call later when he could talk to a secretary and with shaking hands settled the phone back onto its cradle.

Maybe Phil wouldn't call. I hyped myself up to accept that unlikely supposition. Maybe he wasn't as deadly as we'd feared and had already received his kicks out of keeping us on edge.

But I didn't believe that story for a minute. By coincidence a similar drama had played itself out in our newspapers the previous two weeks. A reporter from Chicago was contacted anonymously by a telephone caller who threatened violence to strangers. The reporter's national columns were then devoted exclusively to tense negotiations between the psychotic man and himself, and after he had talked the caller into giving himself up for treatment, police speculated in print on how tragically the story would have ended if the man hadn't been stopped.

I noted marked similarities between that case and this one. Psychiatrists all over the country offered their professional

---

1. The name has been changed to conform to agency confidentiality.

opinions that the Chicago man hadn't been bluffing. Agency officials were convinced that our man wasn't bluffing either. His scheme was too well planned and too graphic.

I'm glad the lines were not busy that morning. It gave me uninterrupted opportunity to pray.

I had welcomed my assignment at Suicide Prevention from the beginning as an answer to our prophet's encouragement to become involved in worthwhile community projects, and I soon found that then, probably more than at any stage of my life, I was conscious of direction. I had the distinct impression that the Lord and I were in partnership in an important endeavor.

Callers seldom stated their real problem. They called for assistance, but they talked in circles. Sometimes the real problem was too painful for them to admit. It became gratifying to note how often I was stumped, only to have a question or comment suddenly pop into my mind that, when articulated, opened up the discussion to new depths, allowing the caller freedom to explore the real hang-up honestly and come to grips with conclusions he or she could live with.

I didn't fool myself that these random ideas came because of my enormous expertise. I knew where they originated and gave credit where credit was due. And if ever the Spirit had indeed occupied the chair beside me, I beseeched its presence that day.

The phone rang. I *knew* who it was. I answered, as usual, *"Suicide Prevention. May I help you?"*

The voice on the other end truly was beautiful, as I had been told it was. Deep. Resonant. Being a choir director, my first irrelevant reaction was to wonder if he sang.

He said pleasantly, *"Good morning! Do you have a calendar handy? Do you remember what day it is?"*

My heart jumped wildly and thundered against my ribs. I doubted that I could summon enough breath to answer. My teeth set up an uncontrollable chatter. I propped an elbow against the desk and rested my quivering chin on its open palm in an attempt to curb their chattering and said, *"Let's see. It's Monday . . . I believe it's about the fifteenth."*

Novices who have not dealt with suicidal persons before might take comfort from the sense of quiet calm in voices of those who have definitely concluded to end their lives. Experienced counselors realize that calm is one of the most unnerving signs of all. Before the decision is finalized, there might be confusion, crying, or hysteria. Once a plan of action is irrevocably established, the need for confusion is gone.

We talked for close to an hour with no lessening of my tension. He told of bitter hatred for his dead parents and for mankind in general. Hunger for something basic that he had missed—or that life had cruelly wrested from him—flowed hauntingly between his words, and it was clear he needed someone to understand.

Once or twice he was on the verge of ringing off. I managed to rechannel his thoughts and hang on to him.

My eyes darted to the typed note hanging on the bulletin board in front of me at eye level:

Never give Phil the impression you are telling him what to do. His instances of violence follow someone suggesting a course of action. He likes to be in command.

Some of his victims had been selected for real or imagined offenses. His comments led me to believe the governor of the state might be his principal target, and Phil just might make it. He was clever and had spent a year weaving and then tightening his strategy.

Others would be taken at planned random at predetermined places. Their only crime would be standing in the right place at the wrong time.

The amount of nervous energy expended in this type of unrelieved tension is inexpressibly draining. In my mind's eye, I watched innocent men and women—and possibly children—dressing to leave home. Unless I quickly came up with a miracle, this would be the final time that ritual was performed. And I seemed to be fresh out of miracles.

*"What can I say to him? What? Help me, Father! Please
don't let my lack of ability contribute to their deaths!"*

While I entreated the Lord for help, Phil proudly related his
admiration for the Texas student some years before who
climbed the university campanile and gunned down everyone
within range of his bullets. That man was Phil's hero, and his
unspeakable stunt was an act of heroism and courage. That
man's name would live forever. It was carved into history for
generations to come. He didn't live and die unnoticed, and in
the long run that's all that mattered.

Phil's explanations droned on and on and his attitude was
that of a kindly master teacher generously imparting his store
of life's hidden mysteries to the impressionable student at his
feet.

I got an idea. It was hazy, and the direction it would lead us
wasn't clear, but it was someplace to start. My eyes fell once
more on the warning not to offer him suggestions. I realized it
was dangerous, but it was my last resort and worth a try. I
couldn't keep him on the phone much longer; clearly the
fateful hour had come. I took a deep breath and dived in.

*"I remember that student, but I don't understand his
motivation. Maybe you can help me, Phil. Do you have any
idea why he did what he did? What do you suppose he was
thinking?"*

He answered importantly as one who is finally in charge
and knew it: *"Oh yes, I know exactly. They performed an
autopsy on his brain after he was dead. They found a brain
tumor."*

Click! There it was, my key to helping him if only I could
do it skillfully. Success or failure rested on my ability to make
contact with whatever rational part of his thinking still existed.

I let him continue his explanations while I hunted for just
the right place to intrude. It came.

"Phil," I interrupted casually, *"the most interesting idea
occurs to me. Probably nothing to it, but you have so much in
common with that student. Your reactions are so similar and
you tell me his were caused by a brain tumor.*

"Have you ever had a complete physical? It's beside the point now, of course, but I'm curious. You've mentioned wide mood swings and your inability to control your temper. Do you suppose it's possible something physical could be influencing your decisions?"

Total silence. Now I'd really done it, I thought, but I was silent also, waiting him out, expecting that at any second the dam of his hair-trigger self-control would explode with a roar.

He was obviously deep in thought when he finally did speak. *"I guess that's possible,"* he said slowly and deliberately. *"It would be interesting to find out, but it's too late. I'll be dead in another hour.*

"I'd look like a fool if I didn't go through with my plans," he continued. *"All of you down there would laugh at me. I've announced my intentions for a year now, and it's all set to go. My files are ready and the tapes are recorded. I've even left instructions where to send them after it's over. I've got to do it today."*

Another silence, shorter this time. I could hear his breathing and feel the pounding of my heart. *"But you're right about one thing—it would be fascinating to know before I go."*

I laughed lightly, which wasn't easy to pull off. He had no way of suspecting how well I understood his fury at manipulation. Trying to sound as off-hand as if suggesting a stroll to the corner grocery, I offered, *"Phil, I don't know about you, but my personality doesn't take kindly to people telling me what to do. If I wanted to learn something vital about myself, I'd like to see anyone stop me. So what, if some of them expect you to act in a certain way; and so what, if they've decided it has to be today! I'd tell them to drop dead* [whoops! bad choice of words] *and take time to check it out for myself."*

I dropped that thought and didn't leave him time to formulate an argument against it. I hurried on to the next step and continued doubtfully. *"But those physicals are pretty expensive. Maybe it isn't practical for you to have one. Do you have enough money?"* (Again, he wasn't aware I knew of his hospital connections.)

So he was able to explain to me in expansive detail how wrong I was and convince me he was capable of working it out. Through his place of employment he was entitled to free medical care. He had never taken advantage of that right to request a full physical but it was within his options and he would consider it.

The pace of his comments had picked up and the smooth sureness was missing from his voice. In its place I heard some quality I couldn't label completely, except for the prominent hints of excitement and curiosity.

He wouldn't *promise* to see a doctor, but he agreed to give it some thought.

I sagged against the desk with relief. He didn't know it yet, but at that moment all of us had won. He was a supremely intelligent man. In spite of warped thought processes, a door had been knocked ajar and he couldn't close it without examining what lay on the other side.

He *would* consult a doctor. And whether his violence was caused emotionally or was the result of some physical mal-function, doctors would have an opportunity to diagnose and treat it.

For the moment, however, he couldn't leave me without a final show of bravado. He hung up saying, *"I'm not promising, you understand. Watch your paper and keep the radio on. Chances are that you and the rest of the world will hear from me real soon!"*

But we didn't. We listened to the radio all that day and the next, but his threats didn't materialize.

What did the doctors uncover? A brain tumor? Severe diabetes? A debilitating thyroid deficiency? We will never know, and it really isn't important to find out.

What is important is that because of the intervention of the Spirit, many people who might not have been are still alive today—and are blissfully oblivious to the fact that their lives were ever threatened.

8
The Intrusion

Bishop Harold Malan yawned as he steered his car to the curb of a neat little tract house on a quiet street in San Antonio, Texas. He was tired. It was close to midnight and he'd put in a long, hard day.

He looked up at the house intently before he got out of the car. The lights were on but everything else seemed to be in order.

A young woman member of his ward he figured to be about twenty-eight or thirty lived inside with her husband and three small children ranging in age from a toddler to a six-year-old, except that she and the children were alone now. Her husband was an officer with the armed forces and he'd been on duty overseas for eight or nine months.

The plucky young mother handled being alone and filling dual roles as mother and father fairly well, all things considered. She was intelligent and capable and well thought of in the community, and in spite of her loneliness there was a plus side Harold had detected in those months without her husband. She'd come to lean more and more on her Heavenly Father. With his help and her own native resourcefulness, she managed the rough spots quite nicely.

That was why the bishop was surprised to be roused from sleep by her frantic call for assistance. She was apologetic for bothering him at that late hour and didn't know quite how to explain, but she knew that someone, or some *thing*, was hiding in her house. She was paralyzed with fear. Would he please hurry over?

He might not have taken her as seriously as he did, except that he had had contact with paralyzing fear. While serving as Chief of Dental Services for the Air Force on the island of Guam, he had arrived home late one night to an overpowering influence of evil hovering at his wife's bedside.[1]

He knew from sober experience how real that presence was and how excruciatingly terrifying, and if there was the slightest possibility that the process was being repeated in a home under his jurisdiction, he wanted to check it out.

The woman opened the door before the echo of his knock died away, and her wide, frightened eyes met his with a look of gratitude. She was shaking, holding on to self-control with a concentrated effort.

On Guam he hadn't seen the spirit that was visible to his wife's eyes, but without a word from her he had sensed its presence.

Here he sensed nothing. He searched the house for a live intruder. He checked locks on windows and doors, looked under beds and behind clothes hanging in the closets. He tip-toed through each room quietly so as not to disturb the children, but when he reached their bedroom, they were wide awake. They huddled under their covers and their little bodies shivered with fright.

He tried to reassure the distraught mother as he tucked the children in snugly. Then he knelt with her in the living room in prayer, where he rebuked whatever unrighteous influence it

---

1. See chapter 14 of the author's book *No Greater Love*, Deseret Book Co., 1982.

was that might be annoying her. Not knowing what else to do, he left, promising he would check on them in the morning.

He was almost back to sleep when the bell on the telephone rang out shrilly at five minutes past one. Harold sighed himself awake and reached for the receiver.

"Bishop Malan!" the woman's voice cried. "Something terrible is here with me in this house. I know it is. Please come back. Hurry!"

He dragged his protesting body from its warm bed, dressed, and drove across town for the second time. He searched the house even more carefully, including the back porch. Nothing.

Once more they prayed together. He urged her to go to bed and get some sleep. He left again, promising to check on her the next morning.

It was after 3:00 A.M. when the phone rang for the third time. Now it wasn't only his weary body that drooped with exhaustion, but his patience was wearing thin. Not quite awake, he mumbled hopefully, "Maybe it isn't necessary that I come personally. Perhaps I can command whatever it is over the phone."

He had reckoned without his good wife, Alta. Over the phone, indeed! In less time than it takes to tell, he found himself out of bed and driving swiftly through the cold night air in a direction that was becoming all too familiar. He hoped it was for the last time that night.

Hurrying across the lawn, he stopped under a maple tree to bow his head. "Father," he pleaded, "open my eyes to the problem here, that I may properly fulfill my calling as spiritual father and protector of the ward."

Instantly—*instantly*—he plunged into darkness so deep and consuming that he could scarcely breathe. It was as if he had tumbled into an unlighted abyss so deep that even the hope of light could not penetrate.

Now he understood the problem. This was the same, unspeakable force he had fought against in the South Pacific.

No one forced him to go into that maelstrom. It requires a special brand of courage to deliberately pit oneself against a

raging force of vitriolic hatred such as the one he knew he
would meet on the other side of the front door, especially
when one faces it for the second time and has no illusions
about its reality. But Bishop Malan believed that the priesthood shield he bore was the only power on earth strong
enough to vanquish the evil intruder.

His rap was answered by a woman reduced to hysterics. He
took a deep breath and stepped into the entry, where he was
hit by violence that was almost physical.

There wasn't a sound from the children's room. They had
either fallen asleep or were too terrified to utter a cry.

The unfairness of the assault angered Bishop Malan to the
extent that it overturned a portion of his fear. Raising his voice
like an avenging angel, he rebuked the awesome tormentor
and commanded it, in the name of Jesus Christ, to leave its
innocent victims in peace. He ordered it to return to the
darkest regions of hell where it made its home and made it
crystal clear that his command covered every nook and cranny
of the house itself and every foot of the property which
surrounds it.

As instantly as its existence had been made known to him,
so it vanished. Like a swimmer caught in the vortex of a
whirlpool that suddenly drains away, his unsteady legs braced
against the release of resistance. His companion sagged and
would have fallen if he hadn't caught her and eased her to a
chair.

He was in no hurry to leave this time. Sleep was the last
thing on his mind. In the midst of the sweet peace surrounding them, his anger remained. He had fought a difficult battle
but he didn't plan to return to his bed until he was convinced
that the retreat of the enemy was permanent.

A slight rustling sound alerted his heightened awareness.
Skipping down the hallway on slippered feet came the two-
year-old, dressed in her warm, flannel pajamas, her footsteps
absorbed by the soft carpet.

She pattered into the living room and threw her arms comfortingly around her mother. "Don't worry, Mommy," she crooned. "Those bad men are all gone."

Harold left then. He went back out into a night that was approaching dawn, but he didn't mind. He knew that for the short part of the night that remained, he would sleep well.

9
The Pulpit-Thumping Preacher

The South is America's Bible Belt and it receives more than its share of pulpit-thumping traveling preachers who breathe fire and brimstone.

Tom McKinney tries to avoid controversial meetings. He was busy at work when his wife called, and Carol was upset. Returning home from an errand, she had driven past a prominent billboard proclaiming for all to see:

EXPOSÉ OF MORMON DOCTRINE

The time was listed as seven-thirty that evening.

The billboard advertised the address of a new Pentecostal church in Bremen, Georgia, and named a professional anti-Mormon minister as guest speaker. Tom was familiar with the man's name but he had never heard him speak.

Bremen is a small mill town sixty miles west of Atlanta, famous for the manufacture of men's shirts and suits.

Tom was curious. He called the Bremen area missionaries and found they were very much aware of the exposé. Two of their serious investigators were members of that church and they had asked the missionaries to be with them to help sort out truth from falsehood. The Elders had agreed to go. Tom decided to join them.

An audience of approximately one hundred persons had already chosen seats in the large, semi-circular chapel when they arrived. Tom and his little group settled down in the third row.

They bowed their heads while a solemn prayer was offered and then the speaker arose.

He was forty-five to fifty years old, about five-feet-nine inches tall, with thinning brown hair streaked with gray, and his distinct English accent seemed to lend a cultured air of authority to his remarks.

Tom was aghast. He thought he had prepared himself to handle whatever he might hear that evening, but he was mistaken. Nothing short of being there in person could have prepared him for the vehemence of the attack.

For one and a half hours he cringed under a ruthless barrage of misquotations, quotations out of context, half truths couched in inflammatory language, and outrageous, bald-faced lies.

Latter-day Saints were described as demons. The speaker assured his rapt audience that Mormons consider Jesus Christ as merely an elder brother, not as the Lord God Almighty. Blasphemy! Not deigning to worship him as he is, Mormons can have no personal relationship with him and hence are doomed. (He neglected to mention that the full name of the Church is The Church of Jesus Christ of Latter-day Saints.)

Knowing full well they will soon be committed to hell (he continued), they are no better than the imps of Satan, and they like nothing better than to drag others down with them.

Masters of persuasion, he screamed, warming to his

subject. Dangerously, diabolically clever! Tragically easy to
believe! Therein lies the secret of their cunning. Their doc-
trines sound so logical!

"Good people of Bremen," he shouted, "protect your
families! Mormons must not be allowed to speak. Decent
people must avoid them like the plague, and that is your only
salvation!"

His approach displayed venom and unreasoning hatred,
and he consciously worked at instilling fear of the unknown.
He yelled and flailed the air with his fists, striking the podium
repeatedly for emphasis and stomping his feet.

Tom and his friends grew increasingly uneasy as the evening progressed. Colorful denunciations were this man's stock
in trade and his means of livelihood. The more dramatic his
approach, the more inflamed his listeners, the more generous
they were liable to be with their donational offerings. Tom
understood his motivation.

But he remembered back a few short years to the time
when he was not personally familiar with Mormons or Mormon doctrine. The speaker had worked himself into a frenzy.
Would Tom have been taken in by his accusations on an
earlier day?

He looked around. It was impossible to judge the congregation's reactions. Eyes were focused on the man and his
gyrations at the pulpit. All were strangely quiet. Typical Pentecostal responses of *Amen!* and *Hallelujah!* were conspicuous
by their absence. What were they thinking? Blank faces regis-
tered shock, and it was impossible to read them. Was it the
lull before the storm?

Tom turned his attention to Elder Newman, at his side.
Both men were convinced that public argument with radicals
who strike viciously without reason or conscience seldom pro-
duces a desirable result. Truth is not brought to light by con-
tention. They could not allow themselves to be drawn into that
position.

Should they make a run for the door before they were

recognized? Every instinct prompted them to flee from the repulsion engendered there that night.

No! The odious accusations could not be allowed to take root unchallenged in the receptive minds of one hundred people. Something had to be done.

The speaker finished and sat down, mopping his damp forehead with a pocket handkerchief, and the meeting was over.

Tom and the two Elders stood up quietly and moved unobtrusively—or so they supposed—to the speaker's side. He rose to meet them beside the podium, breathing heavily from his exertions and heightened emotionalism.

They didn't notice the congregation leaving their seats to press in close behind them. The fact is they couldn't have left before they were recognized. Some special quality sets Latter-day Saint missionaries apart, and their presence was known from the moment they pushed open the door of the chapel.

They quietly introduced themselves to the minister and requested the courtesy of five minutes at the microphone. He refused point blank. Hadn't they listened to his remarks? Mormons were not to be permitted to speak under any conditions. He faced the audience as they closed in and, feeling they were with him, raised his voice again to its fever pitch.

That was when Tom realized that he and his friends were totally surrounded and greatly outnumbered. He had heard of Elder Rulon Killian, alone on a street corner in Tennessee, surrounded by a mob bent on his destruction.[1] He could almost smell the stench of evil, and for the first time he comprehended the full extent of the terror Elder Killian must have known.

Elder Newman stepped to the microphone without waiting for permission. He bore his testimony. He bore it simply and with dignity, with no fireworks and no theatrics.

He declared in words of soberness that the gospel is true

1. See chapter 11 of the author's book *No Greater Love*, Deseret Book Co., 1982.

and that those with a sincere desire to know God would do well to learn of him from the lips of those who are qualified to teach of his ways.

He held the floor no more than two or three minutes at most. But the comparison between the mindless ravings of the older man and the dignity of Elder Newman was impossible to ignore. He closed with their address and an offer to be of service to anyone who desired to hear what Mormon Elders have to give.

Sometime during those few minutes, the minister melted through the crowd and left.

Tom and the missionaries *were* mobbed between the pulpit and their car, but it wasn't by the mob the preacher had in mind. And later, after intense study to satisfy curiosity that he had initiated, six new converts were baptized into the fold.

10
A Visit
With Grandpa

This is the story of an enduring love between a small boy and his grandfather.

Little Jimmy Stoeltzing was desolate when his grandfather died. After all, how many kids vicariously travel up dense, steamy jungles on the Amazon River searching out undeveloped rubber plantations for a United States rubber company, or interview Eleanor Roosevelt as a Washington, D.C., newspaper correspondent?

Grandpa—Charles Carroll Miller—had been named after one of the signers of the Declaration of Independence, and there was nothing he couldn't do. And his storyteller's knack for sharing took Jimmy right along with him.

Auntie Mame, in the musical comedy of the same name, believed that life is a banquet served up on heaping picnic tables while some timid souls allow themselves to starve. Certainly the fictional Mame did not starve, nor Grandpa Miller, either!

When he died without warning at age sixty-six, the shock of his loss was almost more than his seven-year-old companion could take. All at once life was devoid of its savor. A world without Grandpa was a world without fun.

That was how a subdued Jimmy and his reluctant father came to be bobbing gently up and down in their thirteen-foot Boston Whaler on the northern fork of the American River, upstream from Folsom Dam.

Dick and Judy Stoeltzing have two small boys and they follow a tradition of spending one day per month alone with each son, one on one, doing whatever the boy decides to do, within reason.

On this occasion father and son had come to fish, even though Dad Dick's experience and inclination as regards fish in their native habitat was next to nil.

But Grandpa Miller had been another story. Tucked somewhere alongside his many accomplishments, he'd mastered the fine art of fly fishing. He had been an expert's expert, and once or twice he'd taken his grandson out with him. Jimmy was too young to learn the mechanics of the sport but he loved it, and in his mind it became inseparably connected with the grandfather he loved.

On this particular day, Jimmy chose an activity that represented the man he missed so desperately, but who seemed to be so completely and irrevocably gone from him. He may not have been old enough to put the thought into words, but his choice came as close as he knew how to spending the day with Grandpa.

Just before his unexpected passing, Judy's father had presented Jimmy with a fishing creel and equipment. Until now, there hadn't been time to use it. Dick cast a worried glance at his unusually quiet son as he stowed the new gear in the boat. He wasn't at all sure how successful this outing would prove to be. Both of them lacked the necessary experience. He fervently hoped that he, himself, would be able to figure out the proper end of the pole to cast into the water.

They motored up the river to a likely-looking spot, dropped anchor, and bowed their heads for a short word of prayer. They asked for a safe, enjoyable day and Dick silently prayed that being in Grandpa's favorite atmosphere would somehow lessen the small boy's pain.

They opened the new creel. There, nestled among the lures and reels and other mysterious gadgets lay a slip of white paper. It was a letter from Grandpa, and it began:

Dear Jim:

[Jim. How like Grandpa to address him man to man.]

I hope you will like this fly fishing outfit. It has never been blooded. This means it is brand new and has never been used to catch a fish—only to teach you and your brother, Casey, how to cast an artificial fly so that it will flutter down naturally into a quiet mountain pool.

When you blood this rod for the first time, I hope it will be on a scrappy trout that will give you a good fight. Once you hook him, always hold the tip of the rod high. . . .

The letter continued as a step-by-step guide, a fundamental treatise on the "how-to's" of fishing. It took the uninitiated beginner through every conceivable movement, culminating with pointers of good sportsmanship. It spelled out the number of fish they could legally land and cautioned, even so, never to greedily gather in more than they could use.

It specified tasty foods to combine for breakfast over a glowing campfire, once the fish were caught and were sizzling in the pan. Reading, the two fishermen could almost smell the tantalizing aroma.

They followed each step outlined in the letter, slipped their line into the water and—zing! The bait was swallowed by a most respectable-sized trout before Jimmy and Dick could blink their eyes. They reeled in their prize, attached him to the stringer, put on new bait, and repeated the process five times. Each time, no sooner did the hook cleave the water's surface than an open mouth swooped up out of nowhere to grab it.

The Boston Whaler might have been a marine delicatessen in water filled with ravenous fish waiting in line to sample their free lunch.

Other boats were anchored on the river, and as the Boston Whaler reeled in trout after trout, they edged closer.

But those five gorgeous trout were the only ones caught there that day.

Never again did Jimmy feel so deserted. Grandpa wasn't really gone, you see. Wherever he was, he loved them still. Jimmy could scarcely have been more certain of that if he had peeked underneath the boat and surprised his grandfather threading the trout onto their line.

Two experienced, contented fishermen headed for home in the dusk of the evening. They had prayed for a pleasant day and it had been glorious.

11
The Mountain
That Moved (Almost)

The mountains that range across France, Switzerland, and Italy are rugged. The Alps rise abruptly from level ground to towering peaks, and their twisting hairpin turns are challenging. Gentle, rolling foothills graduating upward are unknown in that part of the world.

Closed in winter when snow blocks their passes, the roads are next to impossible for novices to navigate, even in summer.

My sister Dolores, who prefers to be called Lori, didn't know that.

Lori Hitchcock and her son picked up their shiny new Volkswagon bug at the Brussels Airport in Belgium. They piled a tent and other camping gear in and around the tiny, red automobile and they were ready to go.

Mark had turned eighteen and it seemed to Lori to be the perfect opportunity to spend quality hours alone with him. Another year or less and Mark would be grown up and gone.

Now, while he balanced almost across the tightrope between boyhood and transformation into a man, they would camp along the scenic byways of Europe with time for leisurely conversations and the formation of golden memories neither would ever forget.

This was their first trip to Europe. Neither spoke the languages indigenous to the countries on their schedule, but that didn't worry them. Lori teaches high school math and is trained to be practical. She was confident they could handle what Europe presented.

It was glorious summer! Mark reveled in freedom after high school graduation, and Lori was likewise free to fill her hours as she pleased. Adventure beckoned more compellingly with every turn of the wheels.

A colorful map propped on the dashboard kept them on course. Prominent red lines marked the main, super highways, but those they ignored. They preferred sights that lay off the beaten track.

They wanted to meet farmers toiling in their fields and to listen to street vendors in picturesque villages singing out their wares, peddling hot sausages to be eaten with buns, or chestnuts heated over an open fire.

Single purple lines on the map directed them to the second-best highways. Double purple was reserved for rougher roads, and the yellow line indicated those that were barely passable. They chose the single purple, or second best.

The map guided them reliably through Germany and Switzerland during a succession of exciting days and beautiful nights. They marvelled at small haystacks individually perched on short wooden poles in fields resembling a horde of invading Martians. Once they pulled off the road to savor fresh peanuts thrown into a homemade kettle and swirled through hot, bubbling toffee. Europe was everything they had hoped for.

Eventually they reached the foot of the towering French Alps and looked *straight up*. Their breath caught in their throats. To reach Italy they had to cross the mountains. Their map had proved to be a trustworthy guide so far, and their transportation had hummed along merrily as a new car should. They decided together to push on. They pointed the nose of the Volkswagon up and stepped on the gas.

Lori was driving that day. They rose swiftly and safely, and several hours later they were nearing the top when the road began to narrow. By then the view back down was breathtaking.

The narrowness of the road surprised them as the fair-sized highway dwindled to a small trail and finally became two faint tracks. Grass and weeds grew between the tracks, and judging from their undisturbed condition, the trail wasn't often used.

Mark voted to turn around. Lori was tempted, but they had come so far. Surely the road would broaden on the other side of the summit. She drove on.

The trail wound them through the middle of an unkempt yard surrounding a decrepit old farmhouse, the first sign of habitation they'd seen for miles. Chickens squawked and flapped their wings and pigs squealed as they raced out of sight underneath the ancient porch. It wasn't an inviting place to stop, even for a moment. Lori decided to go a little further.

Before long she realized her decision had been a mistake. Rounding a corner, they found themselves perched on a ledge barely wide enough to hold the car. Rough rocks scraped the paint from the door on her side, and Mark looked out of his window onto a dizzying drop of hundreds of feet.

Lori slammed her foot on the brake pedal and stopped. Now there was no room to turn around, and the prospect of backing even a few feet down that narrow ledge caused her heart to flutter uncontrollably.

Mark, with the absolute assurance of inexperience, said crisply, "Give me the wheel, Mother. I'll get us out of here!"

They changed places without leaving the car, because there was no room to stand on either side. Mark slipped the gears into reverse and cramped the wheel all the way to the left. He

gunned the motor and whipped the little bug in a backwards
circle at full speed. Miraculously they skimmed the cliff's edge
without going over, but a resounding crash announced that the
car's rear end and the mountain had tangled and the mountain
had come up winner.

Their tailpipe was wedged tightly between two deeply
embedded rocks, while the front bumper dangled over thin
air. Front tires teetered on the last few inches of firm ground,
threatening to slip over the edge at any moment. Lori's first
thought was to wonder exactly how many miles they were
from home.

Gingerly they eased their doors open, stepped out, and took
stock of the situation. No problem, Mark assured his anxious
mother. He would simply dig the tailpipe out of the mountain
with the handle of their new jack.

There is a universal, indisputable law—Murphy's law—that
applies to situations like this and is dedicated to the proposition that if anything more *can* go wrong, it inevitably *will*. A
search of the trunk revealed that the factory had goofed. The
jack was there but its handle was missing. Now even Mark
knew panic.

Sounds of running feet interrupted their uneasy thoughts
as, huffing and puffing, two men and a woman panted their
way around the bend. The older man came with a shovel slung
over his shoulder.

Did they live in the broken-down farmhouse? Probably, but
there was no telling for sure, since they spoke only French,
while Lori and her son knew no French. They knew the area
well, apparently, and had come prepared to help.

The woman was more agitated than Lori was, if possible.
She threw her arms around Lori's neck and with much
clucking and patting offered what consolation she could.

The older man moved at once to the car and ineffectually
hacked at the mountainside with his shovel. The rocks were
buried too deeply to be removed. Clearly that was not the
answer to their dilemma.

Up to that point Lori had thought things were as bad as they could get. But then the younger man took action. He strode purposefully in their direction and with broad, expansive gestures let them know he wanted them back inside the car. Mark should steer while the man and his family pushed the car forward. They could tell his intentions without a common language, but they were not able to make him understand that his plan had one serious flaw: If the car moved forward, there was no place to go but straight down.

Lori peered over the edge of the cliff. She imagined she glimpsed their unidentified, bleached bones lying halfway down, drying in the summer sun. Surely the poor man must be demented. At the very least, he was determined.

Lori was familiar with the story of the biblical grain of mustard seed, the one that could move mountains, but she had never pictured her own faith being subject to the same test.

Never before had she uttered so fervent a prayer or packed so much solid conviction into so few seconds. There wasn't time to be flowery. As the man pressed toward them, all the spiritual power she possessed went from her in one silent scream for help.

Not ten seconds later they heard the pulse of an approaching engine. Around the same bend they had just traversed roared a big blue van carrying six men. Six husky men. The van screeched to a halt and the doors on both sides flew open. All six hurtled out.

The men were dressed in work clothes and appeared to be workers on their way to a construction job, perhaps unfamiliar with the territory and confused by the same map that had led the Hitchcocks astray.

They swooped down on the trapped automobile. With three on one side and three on the other, and as gracefully as if they were part of a choreographed dance routine, they bent, lifted, and pulled. In unison they freed the tiny car and turned it around to face the direction whence it had come. Without a glance at anyone and without a word they hurried to their van and in a flurry of dust and smoke disappeared down the road as mysteriously as they had come.

Lori and Mark were stunned. This was a solid, real-life answer to Lori's prayer for help, but they had no notion of where the men hailed from or what language they would have spoken *had* they spoken. And the Hitchcocks didn't stick around to try to figure it out. They jumped in their own car, and before the last vestiges of dust from the van had settled to the ground, they were gone.

Lori can laugh now as she recounts the experience, but behind her shaky laughter lies profound gratitude. She learned something valuable that day: Faith put to the ultimate test is a force to be reckoned with.

It may not have been the mountain that moved, but it was close enough.

12
The Unifying
Force

When one thinks of a leader, one tends to picture a man or woman who has lived a fair number of years. Perhaps he or she has a touch of gray at the temples or at least a few lines of wisdom crisscrossing the brow.

But we in Fair Oaks, California, learned in 1972 that there are leadership qualities more important than age.

Steve Smith, Dave Williams, Jeff Perkins and Steven Seither were sixteen when they were called into leadership positions in the Aaronic Priests Quorum, and they took their responsibilities seriously.

They were lively, fun-loving boys who enjoyed parties and a good time, and their bishop was adept at combining the best qualities of worship and fun.

On Sunday evenings they sat in his sunken family room, informally lounging on his thick, spongy carpet, and their discussions were both interesting and deep. Out of those informal gospel lessons grew stronger testimonies and the desire to dedicate themselves to the cause of righteousness. Taking responsibility on their own shoulders instead of waiting for someone older to take the lead became important to them.

Fenton Williams had some remarkable qualities. During his tenure as bishop, no member of his ward was forgotten. He invited us into his home for evenings of games and congeniality which brought us closer as a people. The games were fast-paced and enjoyable, but before his laughing guests said goodnight and drifted away, the bishop made sure our conversations moved to true, faith-promoting experiences. Our ward children were raised in that atmosphere.

So the young leaders worried about one member of their quorum. "Joe" had been baptized with his parents, but he never considered himself to be a worthwhile part of the ward family. Serious problems with drug abuse contributed to his feelings of alienation.

One Sunday three of the young leaders visited with Joe. They drove him into the countryside and parked next to a peaceful wooded area. There they found they could talk to him, and in that setting he could respond.

They expressed their concern and he was deeply touched. When they invited him to join them in prayer, he accepted.

The beautiful clearing they chose was underneath leafy boughs of sheltering trees, and the sun glancing through the leaves seemed to shimmer with holiness.

Joe's eyes filled with tears as his friends pleaded with the Lord to touch Joe's heart and give him strength to overcome his weakness. On their knees they laid plans to fast together. It was a wonderfully uplifting experience for all of them.

Three elated young men dropped Joe off at his home and drove on to a fireside. They were late and the meeting was almost over. They declined the usual refreshment of cookies and punch, and word swept the room that they had begun an important fast. They were surprised at the number who wanted to join in.

Someone suggested it should be a ward youth project, but organization of that magnitude takes time. Fasting could be delayed until Monday morning and continue until Tuesday at dinnertime.

The girls chattered in busy, excited little groups, assigning hamburger and hamburger buns, pickles, catsup and mustard. Their fast would be broken at five o'clock Tuesday evening with a party. Three could bring electric griddles and three more would furnish cake. Two boys volunteered to donate drinks. A telephone committee was established to spread the news.

The original three felt uneasy. They weren't sure that the group as a whole was up to such an undertaking. Teenagers are notoriously hearty eaters with growing bodies. When one meal is skipped, they suffer uncomfortable pangs of hunger. These people were talking two days! Were they biting off more than their bodies could chew?

Our ward had boasted—up until that night—pretty typical teenagers. We were proud of them but recognized they had varying degrees of dedication and sensitivity to each other. Occasional minor frictions between some of them were not serious, but those occasions worried their adult advisers.

Human nature in any group relegates one or two unfortunates to the fringes of the popular inner circle. Our group had its share of those.

The prevailing enthusiasm was contagious, however, and this project caught their imagination. What started as a simple effort by dedicated leaders blossomed spontaneously into a powerful unifying force, and it welded the group into one tight, cohesive unit.

Monday night was family home evening, but even so, Fair Oaks telephones were buzzing. A surprising number of young people had succeeded in fasting all day. Callers declared themselves to be "absolutely famished!" but comparing notes definitely helped.

More than one high school teacher would have been
astounded at the thoughts whirling inside heads and hearts of
some of their students that day. Too bad there's no scientific
method for tabulating prayers as they float up from geometry
class or from those racing a bouncing ball down the basketball
court. If prayers were only colored, the air over Bella Vista
High would have taken on an attractive, rosy hue.

The students were hungry, to be sure, but they would
starve to the death rather than give in to their appetites.
Fasting was a taxing exercise in self-discipline, but they were
doing it together and enjoying their misery to the hilt – their
first exhilarating taste of communal sacrifice that was initiated,
planned, and carried out on their own, and that made it
special.

Tuesday, directly after school, there were phone calls, but
they were more subdued. Initial excitement had given way to a
more thoughtful approach. Personal discomfort took a back
seat as they showed concern for the staying power of their
comrades, and that included everybody.

At four-thirty we watched a parade of weary stragglers
pushing their way up our steep driveway bearing the antici-
pated feast. We felt privileged that our home was the
appointed gathering place.

The fixings were dropped with a thud on our kitchen table.
We plugged their griddles into electrical wall sockets and
promised we would handle arrangements from there on.
Hamburger had already been shaped into patties and we
would fry them to a crispy brown. Condiments lined up along
both sides of the table would be accessible at the zero hour.

Most of the young people didn't hear us. They were
stretched out on the front lawn or had draped themselves
limply across our porch steps.

It required self-discipline on our parts to resist rushing out
to them bearing life-giving snacks, but we restrained those
protective inclinations. We saw beyond their hunger and its
accompanying fatigue. We moved to the door to overhear their

tired comments, and underneath those remarks we glimpsed the spiritual satisfaction they enjoyed.

The moment the upstairs clock chimed five, they deserted the porch and lawns and gathered inside the house.

What a breathtaking sight! A living sea of forty-two solemn teenagers knelt elbow-to-elbow and heart-to-heart across our dining room floor with their heads bowed. They filled the living room to overflowing; spilled out into the entry hall; and splashed up the winding staircase.

My husband and I knelt down on the living room thresh-hold because there was no unoccupied space between them.

One young fellow acted as voice, and he offered up a prayer so profound we would have supposed it to be beyond his years or his youthful understanding. The waiting hamburgers and gnawing hunger pangs were forgotten. The young people were receiving important nourishment to their souls.

The strengths Joe gained that day were impressive, but he eventually regressed and drifted back to old friends and his former life-style.

Was that combined suffering for nothing? Emphatically no! Growth for the forty-one others was permanent and went far beyond assistance to one individual, important as that effort was.

Those few days of strength and unity set up patterns of behavior that would affect their lives and filter down to the homes they expected to establish for their own children.

Some who had toyed with inactivity fulfilled honorable missions subsequent to that day and returned to marry in the temple. Others are now elders quorum presidents or members of bishoprics, Relief Society leaders, and Primary presidents.

They continued to function as a close-knit unit while they were together, and now, scattered to far places, they keep in touch. They are truly "brothers and sisters."

Fenton Williams, Jr., was released as our bishop, but we still like to gather at his home. Sometimes when talk turns to heartwarming true experiences, as it invariably does, we think of Nephi.

He began the account of one difficult period in his youth by saying, "I, Nephi, being exceedingly young. . . ." (1 Nephi 2:16). A day or two later the episode ends: "And now I, Nephi, being a *man*. . . ." (1 Nephi 4:31).

We identify with Nephi. Possibly he wasn't specifically implying a jump to manhood in those few short days, but we parents watched our children turn into responsible, caring adults, and that—certainly—happened almost overnight.

13
The Peace That
Passes Understanding

Marilyn Heward woke from sleep with bitter, salty tears coursing down her cheeks. The nightmare had been so vivid!

She thought she stood in the ward Relief Society room near Burley, Idaho. Sprays of beautiful flowers and lush green plants filled the room and transformed the spot into a garden.

She turned her head to admire the simplicity of a casket that dominated the area, then allowed her eyes to sweep casually over the features of the woman who slept there.

The tranquil face radiated peace, but Marilyn wasn't prepared to accept that. The woman inside the coffin was her mother!

She was awake now, but every aspect of the scene was etched indelibly into her memory. With eyes either open or shut she couldn't block out the casket or the flowers or the softness of the white dress with its delicate touches of lace.

Marilyn was a married woman with small children, but she and her mother shared a special relationship. She simply couldn't think of life without her best friend next door, available for the countless times when she needed her.

Virgel Dana was Marilyn's mother; she was also my favorite aunt.

I think of color when I think of her. I was six years old and she was eighteen when Uncle Leslie introduced us before they were married, and I was completely captivated. I had never seen anyone so beautiful. I remember her then in sparkling shades or rich browns and tans.

When I was twelve, Virgel and Les lived on a farm in Cache Valley, Utah, and she was her community's Queen of the Rodeo. She rode a powerful smoky-white horse in the parade and his tail dusted the ground with each prancing step. Her blouse was made from magenta satin. Its fluorescence set off her luminous brown eyes and creamy complexion.

Life changes all of us. Health problems robbed Virgel prematurely of the vibrant color of her eyes and hair. Her skin grew pale and she looked tired.

Marilyn shook herself awake. The dream was obviously related to her mother's checkup at the hospital the next day and was a trick of her subconscious. She pushed it resolutely to the back of her mind while she scolded herself for being so foolish.

She and her husband, Max, visited Virgel in the hospital room the next evening. The news wasn't as pleasant as they'd hoped to hear. Surgery was necessary, and it was already scheduled.

The operation went very well, and Virgel came out of the effects of the anesthetic ahead of schedule. But unexpectedly, in the process of being lifted from the gurney to her bed, she suffered heart arrest and sank into irreversible coma.

All that day Marilyn stood at the waiting room window staring out with unseeing eyes, hoping and praying, willing her mother to fight to live and explaining to the Lord how badly she needed her.

Friday ebbed slowly away and merged into the early morning of Saturday. In those long hours of waiting, her prayers changed. She stopped demanding unconditionally that her mother live, and she began to ask for courage. Gradually she came to accept the fact that she must permit what was best for her mother, whatever that might be.

From that state she progressed to pleading with all her heart for the strength it appeared she might need.

At 4:30 P.M., the hospital intercom bristled: "ICU, Stat!" She didn't have to be told what it meant. Her mother was gone.

But true to Virgel's personality in life, somehow she managed to stay until her daughter could face what a few hours earlier would have been her undoing.

New strength carried Marilyn home to explain to her little ones that the grandmother they idolized wasn't coming home. It sustained her through handling funeral arrangements in order to ease the shock for her father. She comforted friends who came to her and cried with the grief of their own loss.

The details of the dream didn't enter her mind until she walked into the mortuary to select a casket. In a large room filled with dozens of styles to choose from, the difficult decision was made for her. Over there, waiting in the corner, was an exact replica of the one she had seen in her dream.

Quickly she asked to see a dress. The attendant suggested she try elsewhere because his supply at the moment was limited. He had only two dresses on hand. Marilyn insisted he produce them.

Needless to say, one of the gowns was identical to the dream dress, and the size could have been custom tailored to fit her mother.

Prophetic dreams fill various needs. Marilyn's provided comfort. She hadn't been prepared to accept or understand its message of peace at the time, but now the memory of the dream returned to give her strength. She walked out of the mortuary knowing that she would miss her mother every day of her life, but now she could accept the temporary separation.

Death is part of the plan of life, and her mother was in good hands. A compassionate Father who notes the fall of each tiny sparrow had shown her—in advance of her need—that all things are known to him and that he prepares for the home-coming of those who love him.

Where her mother had gone, she was expected.

14
The Night
Dinner Grew Cold

Laura Whitaker was annoyed. Tonight of all nights her husband, a pharmacist, was slow in coming home from work. They were already a few minutes late for a dinner party, but not yet so tardy that the host and hostess couldn't understand and forgive—if they hurried.

Parties of this sort seldom begin exactly at the appointed hour, and Laura took heart by envisioning other guests still visiting in the living room while food was dished up in the kitchen and placed on the festive dining room table.

Being a few minutes late didn't bother Laura nearly as much as her husband's totally unexpected and irresponsible attitude once he did get home. Instead of flying into the house and discarding jacket and necktie as he raced to the bedroom to change, he stopped short barely inside the front door.

"Honey," be began wistfully, "would you mind if we stop on the way to the party to pick out some baby furniture?"

Laura couldn't believe her ears. The tone of his voice suggested that he wasn't really asking her permission, he was stating a fact. He had already decided, and that wasn't like him. He isn't a flighty, inconsiderate man who disrupts well-laid plans on a whim. Surely he couldn't mean to wander around baby shops while ten or twelve other hungry couples waited for their dinner! Such an act was completely out of character.

She scanned his face anxiously. No, he wasn't joking. He was serious. And not only serious, he was adamant.

Laura and Brent both wanted a baby. Their application to adopt had been filed with the Church adoption services for over a year, but there were no guarantees. Hopefully sooner or later exactly the right child would be located and made available for them, but it might take years or it might never happen. They had planned to remain emotionally uninvolved to guard against being hurt.

Once in a while they saw prospective parents in a movie or a TV play, and this made them ache with anticipation. They were sorely tempted to paper the nursery walls with figures of Bo Peep and Humpty Dumpty, or to set up a crib and cover it with dainty quilts and matching pillow, but they fought back those impulses.

After each temptation, they decided anew that that approach was not sensible. Better to hold off preparations until they were notified.

What had changed? Laura searched Brent's intent face again. No doubt about it—he intended to shop for baby furniture, and it had to be that very minute.

She followed her husband to the car but she didn't go cheerfully. She remembers slamming the car door harder than was necessary and she thinks she may have stomped her feet a bit along the way.

She was embarrassed. What could they say when they arrived at dinner an hour or two late and were greeted cooly by soggy food and irritable friends? How could they justify rude behavior when she couldn't make sense out of it herself?

At the store they settled on a white plastic baby carrier such as infants lie in at public meetings or that parents occasionally place at one end of the dinner table at home so their baby will be companionably close. Then Laura turned to leave.

Brent wasn't through. He was halfway down the next aisle, headed toward an exhibit of infant car seats. Car seats? If a baby were delivered to them tomorrow, it would be months before it needed a car seat.

Laura doesn't recall ever being more confused than she was on that strange night.

Finally the driving compulsion that pushed her husband on appeared to be satisfied. Brent contentedly carried his purchases to the car and stowed them in the trunk, and at last the couple headed for what was left of the evening.

After the party—and the apologies—were over, the boxed furniture was stored away in the garage, and there it remained for quite some time, gathering dust, unopened and unused.

A year had passed. Laura sat at her desk in the family room, sorting out old records to be filed or discarded.

Dawn, their precious baby daughter, was with them and was crawling by then, and she was the center and joy of their existence.

Laura smiled tenderly, watching the baby at play with her toys heaped on the soft carpet. Then she reluctantly pulled her attention back to the stack of invoices on the desk.

Suddenly a familiar date caught her eye. April 10, 1980. She picked the paper up to examine it more closely.

It was the receipt for the baby furniture her husband had insisted on buying on that strange night when puzzled friends waited and the gourmet dinner grew cold.

April 10. They were not aware of it that night and hadn't been officially notified until the middle of May, but April 10 had been one of the most important dates of their lives.

Coincidence that Brent felt compelled to shop on that particular evening? Hardly. Not to those who know Brent and are familiar with his reluctance to cause anyone inconvenience.

A shiver went through Laura's body and for the first time she felt she understood the depths of her husband's spiritual sensitivity and the eternal nature of the bonds of love that attached them to their child.

Brent's overwhelming compulsion to prepare for the arrival of their new child had occurred precisely on the night when she was born.

15
The Dedication

How powerful are prayers of dedication for one's dwelling? Can they really stand firm against ravages of earthly elements of destruction?

Hanover Park, Illinois, is generally a beautiful city with lovely homes. Even so, when Elders Greg Henninger and Dale Ficklin moved into a new (to them) apartment in Hanover Park, they dedicated the premises without delay.

It wasn't strictly necessary, they supposed. Other sets of missionaries had lived in those rooms for a year or more, and the first pair must have dedicated the apartment when they took possession.

Still, there *had* been a short break in missionary occupancy, and they would feel more comfortable if the place were re-dedicated.

They suspected the neighborhood was a little rough. The general area of the city wasn't so bad, but in the few blocks around theirs crime was rampant, it turned out, and getting worse. How bad they had no clear idea until after they settled in.

Ten or twelve apartment buildings huddled closely together facing each other on both sides of the street. The rooms rented by Elders Henninger and Ficklin were in the basement of a structure that stood three stories high. Its outside was beautiful white brick.

Fires broke out around them with alarming frequency, and during the dark hours between midnight and dawn, windows were stealthily broken. Shadowy figures slipped inside through the jagged openings to take their pick of the unfortunate sleeping occupant's choicest belongings. The two Elders had a feeling they could use all the protection they could get.

So they solemnly knelt together in a moment of prayer. They asked the Lord to bless their new home, to make it a place of peace and a refuge from the cares of the world. They requested earnestly that he guard their windows against breakage in the night and allow nothing to damage any part of the apartment's interior.

Contentedly they then arose from their knees.

But outside, the violence continued. Vandalism skyrocketed in the immediate neighborhood, and one night someone shot at their car as they slept.

A night or two later they woke to the wail of screaming sirens. Flames lit up the sky and danced in and out of the building across the street, and by the next morning it was gone —burned down to the ground. Another case of deliberate arson.

That fire was the final straw. That morning their president instructed them to leave the neighborhood at once. Obediently they located another apartment, and with the help of one of the members they removed their few belongings that very day. As they left Apartment 1A for the last time, they closed the door firmly behind them.

Elder Henninger returned to the street with a new companion a few days later. They were tracting. He'd been told the building had burned almost simultaneously with their leaving the premises, and he now stopped by to inspect the damage.

Slowly he walked up the sidewalk toward what appeared to be only an ugly shell. The white bricks were black with soot and the building was gutted.

He picked his way over burned timbers lying helter-skelter across his path and climbed cautiously down to what had once been the level of the basement. The roof had caved in. Looking up, he saw that nothing stood between him and the sky.

He worked his way across charcoal debris to the location of their old apartment. He was surprised to find the front door still upright on its hinges—scorched, but there.

His curiosity got the best of him. Given the total destruction of the other units, he was confident the owner would have no objections to what he planned to do next. He moved closer, raised his right foot, and with a quick thrust kicked the door open. Then he gasped!

The apartment was exactly as it had been when they left it. Not a breath of smoke or fire had entered. The inside of the front door was not singed or blackened, and every window was in place. Not one pane of glass had exploded in an intensity of heat that had shattered every other window in the building.

The apartment had been preserved without blemish despite the fact that the fire had been set directly across the hallway and that the main concentration of heat centered at the apartment level.

With a blinding flash, he remembered their ceremony of dedication.

Later, Elder Ficklin passed by on his way between assignments. He traveled out of his way to see for himself what he'd heard about from his former companion.

He didn't get out of his car; it wasn't necessary. He parked at such an angle that from the automobile's front seat he could observe what he'd come quite a distance to see.

It was true. The apartment stood intact, as alone among the lonely bricks as a beacon light on a hill—an island of peace in a troubled world.

16
Between the Lines

POLAND DEDICATED BY PRESIDENT KIMBALL

Church News, Sept. 17, 1977, Warsaw, Poland:
In a simple but eloquent ceremony, Aug. 24, 1977, President
Spencer W. Kimball dedicated the land of Poland and blessed
its people that the work of the Lord might go forth. . . .
The visit and dedication were made possible by official recogni-
tion of the Church by the Polish government, May 30. . . .

Krakow is a lovely old city of charm and grace in the south-
west corner of Poland.

Most of Krakow's buildings are old and seem to tell of
history. City law stipulates that standing structures may not be
razed until they have served their proper measure of use, and
then the new buildings replacing them must conform to the
architecture of the buildings being torn down. The city is
sometimes affectionately described as one giant museum.

Thus the Polish people's love for their heritage is maintained. Another part of that heritage is their intense love of
freedom, which has been maintained over the centuries.

My friend Max Lieber is a chemical engineer from Switzerland who deals in plastics.[1] He travels on occasion to various fairs and exhibitions around Europe. This time he had taken his wife, Suoma, along with him.

The Liebers planned to spend a weekend in historic Krakow, and they were now seated in the hotel's gracious dining room, mapping out a schedule for the following day's sightseeing.

A personable young fellow dressed in a formal tuxedo identified himself—in flawless German—as their waiter for the evening. Which language would they prefer him to speak?

Fluent in several, they offered *him* a choice: German, English, French, Finnish, or Swiss dialect would be fine. He chose English because the chance to practice that language didn't present itself every day. A language major, he modestly insisted he needed the practice, but his English too was beautifully articulated.

Max and Sue finished a leisurely dinner. Sue nibbled on her last few crumbs of dessert while Max signaled for the check.

They weren't offended when their waiter politely questioned them. They were accustomed to sensing curiosity as they travelled. Why hadn't they drunk the usual cocktail before dinner, or coffee, tea, or wine with their meal, or sipped a liqueur afterwards, or smoked a cigar or cigarette with dessert? This curious onlooker meant to find out the reason for their rejection of the "good things" of life.

Patiently they explained that their religion made them different. He'd never had religious training and had never heard of Mormons. He could understand lip service to a religion that demanded sacrifice, but the Leibers were so many miles from anyone who would recognize them. What manner of belief could evoke that type of allegiance and self-discipline?

---

1. See chapters 17 and 18 of the author's book *No Greater Love*, Deseret Book Co., 1982.

Intrigued, he asked a number of significant and searching questions.

One of the questions was whether the Liebers had any literature about their beliefs. When he travels, Max carries the pamphlet of the Joseph Smith story in his jacket pocket, and he now brought it out. The questions continued, and the more the young man asked and was answered, the more he hungered to know.

He suggested a fair exchange. The next day was his day off. If they wanted to see the real Krakow, the one the normal tourist doesn't see, he would guide them—so long as they would agree to exchange with him information about their respective cultures and backgrounds. The Liebers' views intrigued him out of all proportion to the few bits of information he had had time to elicit.

The tour was exciting. It started with a bustling open marketplace called the Rynok. Rising majestically at one corner of the market was the church of three names: Church of Our Lady, Church of Panna Marja, and Church of the Trumpeter, where a trumpeter is eternally on duty to sound a hymn every hour toward all four points of the compass in tribute to another trumpeter killed by the Tartars more than seven hundred years ago.

From the Castle of the Kings high on Wawel Hill they gazed down on the ancient spired city, as beautiful and stately today as it was five hundred years before.

Their guide pointed out Krakow's magnificent monuments to the past and filled their minds with the universal Polish reverence for their ancestors. They could foresee it would be fertile ground for genealogical and temple work that binds family units together for eternity.

Before Max and Sue left town, the three were fast friends. After the Liebers returned to Switzerland, letters were exchanged. The young man's desire for knowledge about their church was insatiable. In due time they invited him to come to their home as a guest if he could make the arrangements, so that they could help him satisfy that desire.

The Liebers felt it would take considerable time to obtain a visa, and they knew that university classes were soon due to begin and that their friend had to be on hand to register. So it appeared to them the visit was unlikely at best. Perhaps next year . . .

But there was one thing they hadn't taken into account. They had reckoned without the Lord. And they didn't know how important the young man was to the Lord's overall blueprint.

Max and Sue received surprising notification that their guest was on his way and would be able to stay for a week. I don't state categorically that they met him on the bottom step of the train with missionaries in tow, but I do guarantee that the Lieber apartment hummed nonstop for the next few days. Eight, ten hours at a stretch the missionaries taught, and the visitor absorbed like a dry sponge that must be filled before it can be put to use.

The night before he boarded the train to go back home, he strode enthusiastically into the waters of baptism. He returned to his homeland a Latter-day Saint.

Percy Fetzer of Salt Lake City didn't know about the activities of the Liebers.

Acting under the direction of David M. Kennedy, formerly United States Secretary of the Treasury and now special representative of the First Presidency, Brother Fetzer had come to Poland as an ambassador for Spencer W. Kimball, President of The Church of Jesus Christ of Latter-day Saints. The Fetzer assignment was to locate eight Polish nationals who were members of The Church of Jesus Christ of Latter-day Saints and obtain their signatures to a document. These signatures were required so that the Church could petition the Polish government for official recognition.

That recognition, the granting of legal status, would mean opening the way for meetings to be held and ordinances to be performed. It would constitute permission to conduct legitimate business with official government sanction. Without permission, the Church was powerless to operate in Poland.

A prophet of God had stated that now was the moment favored by the Lord. Elder Kennedy, experienced in diplomacy and familiar with international governmental negotiations, had already worked with Polish officials to prepare the way for the agreement. But before his impending return to Poland, the necessary paper work must be in order. And Percy Fetzer knew that time was running out.

Brother Fetzer looked down at the document in his hand. It contained the signatures of seven people—many of whom had worked diligently with the government in the effort to have the Church legally recognized in their homeland. Brother Fetzer had worked tirelessly for days, and those seven were all he could find.

Nonetheless, there was a ray of hope. He'd received notification from the Swiss Mission of a recent baptism, and he was looking forward to meeting the new member on this visit. If he could find him, perhaps his could be the eighth signature.

Addresses in Krakow are confusing to foreigners. He was misdirected to the wrong side of town and drove for long, unproductive hours along unfamiliar streets. The sun set and the hour grew late.

At long last he discovered his mistake and made his way to the general area of the address. Every apartment building was identical to its neighbor, and for another anxious period his only rewards were frustration and doubt.

It was eleven o'clock at night when he identified the address. The apartment was dark and still. Was it occupied?

He knocked on the door. Minutes ticked silently by before the door was opened far enough to disclose the quizzical face of a brand new, sleepy convert.

That face was one of the sweetest sights Brother Fetzer's eyes had ever beheld.

. . . The recognition culminated years of waiting and hoping. It was gained by local members who for more than a year worked with government officials, and by Elder David M. Kennedy, special representative of the First Presidency, who visited Poland several times and was able to meet with high Polish officials.

When Elder Kennedy got that document granting recognition, he held onto it like it was gold and he walked two feet off the ground.

—La Varr Webb, *Deseret News* Staff Writer

17
The Unlikely Gift

This is the story of a small cemetery, 1.52 acres in size, nestled quietly on top of a rolling hill (near Sloughhouse, California), green each spring, soon parched brown by the summer sun.

There's more to the story than names and dates on stone. Entwined here are the lives of pioneer settlers, their neighbors, hired hands, Indians, blacks, a Chinese or two, and an occasional traveler who didn't reach his destination. What started out as a final resting place for husbands and children of the Thomas Rhodes family grew to include about three hundred graves.[1]

It was September 1982, and the grounds were brown when I first wandered among the graves. A sense of peaceful serenity is present there, a feeling not of death but of lives lived to the fullest, of stories waiting to be told.

Most of all, the cemetery speaks to me of love.

---

1. Taken from *Historic Cosumnes and the Slough House Pioneer Cemetery*, by Norma Baldwin Ricketts, Daughters of Utah Pioneers, 1978.

The innocence of the marble lamb guarding the grave of one little girl seems to be love personified.

Wrought-iron fences of magnificent design still encircle a few family plots, although vandals have spirited others away. The fences are rusted now, but rust cannot disguise intricate scrollwork nor the obvious desire of the people within those protective borders to be identified—even in death—as family units.

I ran the tip of one finger lightly over a tombstone. Impressive stone markers tower five or six feet tall in some instances and are decorated with elaborate sculpted roses. I wondered at the incredible effort it must have taken to transport the heavy granite to that resting place on the hill.

Some of the names inscribed on those markers are synonymous with early California history—linked with Captain John Sutter and the discovery of gold, which the Rhodes boys flicked out of rocks with the tips of their knives; with the ill-fated Donner Party, most of whom perished in the rugged Sierra Nevada Mountains; and with courageous rescue attempts made by two of the Rhodes brothers.

This, however, is not a chronicle of early pioneer days. Those stories have already been told.

This is a tale of modern times.

If anyone had approached Maurine Smart before 1971 and asked her for a list of unlikely presents she expected to be handed in her lifetime, first on her list (if she'd thought of it) would have been a cemetery. She was speechless when it was offered.

To be honest, it wasn't given to her personally, but it was donated through her to Daughters of Utah Pioneers, Sacramento Camp. She was the current president.

It was owned by Percy Westerberg, a descendant of Thomas Rhodes. Percy had terminal cancer and could no longer be responsible for the upkeep of the cemetery. Maurine and the Daughters cherish historical memorabilia. They agreed to take it over and they christened it Slough House Pioneer Cemetery.

The graves had never been recorded in city, county, or state official archives. Priceless genealogy languished under years of dirt and grime. Knee-high weeds curled tightly through spokes of the beautiful fences and choked off access to the stone markers, so the first order of business of the new owners was to arrange for a day of cleanup.

An army of twenty determined Daughters descended on the hill one sweltering July morning prepared to do battle. Straw hats tied under chins protected them from the heat of the sun, and their weapons were whisk brooms and hoes. Lunchtime sandwiches they carried in brown paper bags.

Maurine set up headquarters on a card table in the center of the arena. She passed out blank mimeographed information forms prepared for the occasion by the group historian. Names and dates etched into headstones had corresponding locations on the slips of paper.

The workers were given clear-cut instructions. They should:

1. Write down *verbatim* the information found on each marker;

2. Place the completed slip on the ground at the base of the stone that furnished the information;

3. Weight the paper down with a rock.

Maurine would pick them up as needed.

Maurine unfolded a large plot plan and spread it out on her table. Each identifiable grave was represented on her map by a corresponding square. At day's end, each square would contain a name, and the data could then be formally recorded. Genealogists would have a rich new source from which to draw.

Some graves would be impossible to identify, she knew. Wooden markers had been swept away by four separate fires, and all traces that they ever existed had been obliterated. Hopefully there were only a few in that category.

Work progressed smoothly. Volunteers moved from grave to grave, leaving completed slips in specified places. Maurine retrieved the papers in proper order and transferred the contents to her chart.

The sun circled higher overhead as they bent over their work and its rays beat down fiercely on the parched ground. The women were uncomfortable but nobody slowed down to worry about it. It was nearly noon.

Maurine was writing, so she didn't raise her head when someone walked to her side. Out of the corner of one eye she noticed two slips deposited on the table, and she frowned. The organized routine worked well and it was established. Why would one of them change the procedure?

"Don't leave slips here," she scolded crisply. "Take them back. I'll pick them up when I need them!"

A restless breeze stirred the papers and they drifted to her feet as she spoke. She bent to pick them up, and with one continuous motion she turned to hand them back to the woman who had brought them.

Her hand stopped in mid-air. No one was there.

She glanced quickly around the cemetery. Every worker was busily engrossed some distance away, pulling weeds, whisking off tombstones, or writing information. Maurine shivered in spite of the heat.

"Yoohoo, ladies!" she called. "Who brought me these slips?" She waved the papers in the air and heads turned briefly in her direction. But no one had been near the table, and they all bent again to their labors.

When the Daughters gathered for lunch Maurine put the question to each of them individually. She passed around the forms, printed in heavy pencil with bold, sweeping strokes:

Family - Wilcox. Adelaide, 14 mos., 10 days.

Family - Wilcox. Katty, Native of Springfield.

The workers were mystified.

The cemetery did hold a Wilcox family plot. It was enclosed within one of the wrought-iron fences. A conscientious worker had carefully transcribed the information on two headstones inside the plot, but there were only two. The names on *her* slips were Lyman and Fanny. There was no indication of anyone else.

Maurine and fellow Daughter Bea Taylor set their lunches aside and stepped to the Wilcox graves. The others followed. They read the tombstones belonging to Lyman and Fanny.

But then they noticed something decidedly out of the ordinary about the way the stones were positioned. They were not centered neatly inside the encircling fence. They stood off center, and the remaining bare ground was exactly the size two small bodies might require if they were placed end to end to be next to their parents.

Yes, the cemetery whispers to me of love and I understand its voice. I stood next to the fence and held the papers in my hand.

Someone—was it a mother, perhaps?—adored those two small babies and even in what we call death couldn't permit them to be forgotten.

18
The Roswell Miracle

Barbara Borg's father, Richard Robinson, arrived for an extended visit at her home near Roswell, Georgia, outside of Atlanta, in late December, 1980. He was with her on January 10, 1981 — groundbreaking day for the proposed new Roswell ward.

Barbara's husband was detained at work that day, so Barbara and her father gladly accepted a ride in the car of two missionaries.

They were a few minutes late but still able to park close to the meeting site, a vacant lot next to the street. They walked approximately twenty yards to the rear of the congregation, moving to strains of the opening song, "The Lord's Prayer."

Barbara noticed that her father appeared to be extra-ordinarily pale. She was asking, "Dad, are you all right? Would you like to sit down?" when he began to fall.

She cried out involuntarily, "Elders!" The heads of two hundred startled members jerked in their direction. Eight missionaries standing nearby caught her father and eased him gently to the ground. He was already dead.

Emotional shock ran through the meeting like a bolt of electricity, and Barbara, of course, was particularly distressed. Her dad had been in remarkably fit condition. She wasn't prepared in any way for this sudden passing.

Two members of the congregation happened to be highly trained in handling this type of emergency and they immediately took charge. Elder Mark Cutting, one of the Elders who lowered Brother Robinson to the ground, responds to casualty calls several times a day at his home in Sydney, Australia, where he works as an ambulance officer. Without hesitation he arranged the body for resuscitation.

Wanda Grindstaff was employed as a nurse in the cardiac care unit of a local hospital. She stooped to begin CPR (cardiac pulmonary resuscitation) but found she couldn't force the depth of compression necessary to circulate blood throughout the body, so the two changed places. Elder Cutting continued CPR and Wanda began mouth-to-mouth.

Barbara's father had been seized with a massive heart attack. That was apparent. His unnaturally pale skin had flamed to red as if with a quick flush or cutoff of circulation, then from red to ominous blue.

The two employed all the medical skill at their command, but to no avail. The truth is that even in well-equipped hospitals with drugs and defibrillator on hand, the percentage of patients brought back to consciousness from apparent death is fractional at best. And they were attempting to save his life in a vacant lot without any modern equipment.

It was the strangest resuscitation attempt either had ever participated in. The body was tense in its bearing. Its unnatural stiffness made it impossible to tilt the head back far enough to allow for free passage of air. The two worked with frantic speed because they knew, of course, that a few minutes without oxygen spells irreversible damage to the brain.

Medical technicians in hospital settings work with every tool at their disposal and sometimes continue their efforts for hours. Suddenly, with no audible word of command, they often give up at the same second. There is no mistaking the emptiness of a body the spirit has abandoned.

So it was with Brother Robinson's body. Wanda states, "Oh, yes. He was unmistakably dead."

Still they continued their efforts, as the distraught onlookers pleaded, "Don't stop! Don't stop!"

In the midst of the confusion, Brother Max Kimball, first counselor in the Sandy Springs Stake presidency and a man known in the area for his deep spiritual nature, left the speaker's platform and made his way quietly through the crowd. The tight circle surrounding the body parted and President Kimball knelt down at his side.

A phial of consecrated oil was produced, and President Kimball and Elder Gregory Robinson administered to the dead man. President Kimball sealed the anointing in his customary, reverent, Brother-Kimball voice. Then he paused. For a moment the air around them was very still.

Then in a deeper, more powerful, more authoritative voice that rang like thunder to listening ears, he said:

"Richard Robinson, by the power and authority of the Holy Melchizedek Priesthood which I hold, I *command* your spirit to return to your body!"

The stricken man took one great, shuddering gasp of air and began to breathe normally. The deathly pallor of his features warmed to a pink, healthy glow. His eyes blinked open. He looked up at the circle of anxious faces hovering over him, and he smiled.

Fearful of brain damage because of the length of time which had elapsed, Wanda called him by name and he responded in a completely lucid manner.

Someone had phoned for paramedics. When their ambulance raced up to the lot with siren shrieking and the stretcher-bearing attendants hit the ground at a run, they wondered why they'd been called. Their patient was so normal in every way they were in no hurry to rush him any-where.

But they escorted him to a hospital to be checked. Once he was admitted, his chief concern was hunger. It was too late for breakfast and too early for lunch, but he finished off a special brunch prepared just for him by an obliging staff—omelet, juice, toast, and sweet roll. He ate it ravenously down to the last delicious bite.

The scriptures record several instances in which people were restored to life by the power of the priesthood. Two hundred people who were on that vacant lot in Georgia testify that that same power still functions today. Now when they meet on that sacred spot, it reminds them they witnessed a miracle.